CW00793791

Memories of
the Gorbals

Also by Jack Caplan

From Gorbals to Jungle

Memories of the Gorbals
by
Jack Caplan

THE PENTLAND PRESS LTD
EDINBURGH CAMBRIDGE DURHAM

© Jack Caplan 1991

Reprinted in 1992 by
The Pentland Press Ltd.
Brockerscliffe
Witton le Wear
Durham

ISBN 1 872795 17 X

Typeset in Times by Print Origination (NW)
Limited, Formby, Liverpool L37 8EG
Printed and bound by Antony Rowe
Limited, Chippenham, Wiltshire SN14 6LH
Jacket design by Geoff Hobbs

In Loving Memory of Mum and Dad.

Jack Caplan's 'Memories of the Gorbals' will give readers an insight into life as it once was in probably the most famous area of Glasgow.

Over the years much has been written about the Gorbals and in his book Mr Caplan tells of life and conditions as they were between the two great wars. It is down to earth, humorous and informative.

The old Gorbals is no more and currently the area is the subject of a planned multi-million pound regeneration project.

It is important that we do not forget the past. Jack Caplan has made sure of that.

The Rt. Hon. The Lord Provost of Glasgow

Mrs Susan Baird CBE OSt.J JP DUniv.

Contents

Preface

The old Gorbals of Glasgow was one of the most depressing but exciting areas in our City Centre of Glasgow and when I travelled through it daily on my way to school as a youngster it appeared to be an area of mystery and gloom. However, within it there was a kind of lifestyle which every sociologist historian should find more fascinating than almost any other area in the United Kingdom.

Jack Caplan's account of the Gorbals as a former resident and small businessman should be a fascinating read for everyone interested in Glasgow, in Scotland, in city life, and in the human personality.

SIR TEDDY TAYLOR M.A., M.P.

Prologue

This is the true story of just one Jewish family who lived in the Gorbals district of Glasgow between the first and second World Wars.

The parents, immigrants from Lithuania – now part of the USSR – settled in that large industrial city of Scotland around 1899.

Morris and Fanny Caplan reared seven children – five boys, two girls – at 77 South Portland Street, situated in the heart of the Gorbals. For the children, these were halcyon days. They could not realise, of course, that in actual fact they had been destined to live through what were perhaps the most depressing years in the history of Britain. Long years of mass unemployment; of hunger, poverty, strikes, riots and, what was even more menacing, a preparation for war by Germany and Italy.

It is Jack, the third youngest – the fourth son – who looks back and gives his impressions of those years that are gone forever, into oblivion.

In the years following the end of the Second World War, the Jews left the Gorbals almost en masse, and another ethnic group filled their place and their old homes: Pakistanis.

A new Gorbals has arisen, like the Phoenix. Its former citizens, Jewish immigrant families – a small ethnic group, but a vital one – has departed into the mists of time, with hardly a sign today of their former presence, like a ship that has passed in the night.

Historians, I hope, will wish to record my kaleidoscopic pictures for posterity. For even I, who lived and loved, played and fought in the streets, am becoming more vague in distinguishing dreams from reality. This is the price we all pay for the passing of the years. Thankfully not yet senile, I retain my memories. In the still of the nights, I make a rendezvous with nostalgia. I can romp with ghosts – the boys and girls of a forgotten era.

My Yiddishy Mama

The voice of the late, great Sophie Tucker, the last of the 'red-hot Mamas' of Hollywood, still rings in my ears. It was she who immortalised the pathos and depth of feeling contained in the song, titled as above. I am not ashamed to admit being overwhelmed with nostalgia and a swelling in the throat on hearing (or even thinking of) that song. Tears well up in my eyes. Confound it! I have to struggle hard in order to control the desire to cry. Sure, I'm a sentimental old fool. What else? After all, I am 75 years of age, a father of four children, and to boot a grandfather of three delightful kids.

Some things in life are inexplicable. I am not referring to the wonders of the universe, or to the workings of the human brain, but merely to the genetical and biological formation of us humans. What makes us tick in so many differing ways? Is it how we respond and react to old melodies and memories from the past? Or why is it that five men, brothers, can all be from the same womb, with the same father too, peas in the same pod (if you prefer that expression) yet can each be quite an individualist in all things, from habits to politics? From the kind of company we keep to the varying taste of the music we choose we differ, not forgetting books (from comics to the classics) and of course WOMEN. On reflection, my brothers and I had this in common – attraction to the opposite sex. But again, some of the ladies whom my brother Sam bedded with . . . well, I would not have touched with a 20 foot pole. To be sure, one man's meat is another's nightmare.

I shall deal with my four brothers and two sisters later. Of necessity, in

1

so doing, it has to be in kaleidoscopic form. To do otherwise, I would require to write in volume in order to do justice to them. Carl and Sam, the elder brothers, specifically, had full and hectic lives: Carl, the intellectual; Sam, the prodigal. Yet, in terms of potential, Sam had a shrewdness and a mind which was akin to an untapped goldmine. Furthermore, he was by far the more colourful character: a delightful rascal is perhaps the best description I can offer at this stage. In my formative years, Sam was my idol. To me he was James Cagney and Edward G. Robinson rolled into one. Tough, quick of temper, a great lover, whose seminal-sac was ever full. But alas! Not the best of sons for any mother.

This section is for my Mum. A dear, wonderful lady who sacrificed all for her children. Her only fault was that she was too saintly, and was thus exploited by too many people, out of greed and lack of consideration for a woman whose life was one of toil and devotion to her family.

Mother spoke Russian, Hebrew and Yiddish. An avid reader of classical literature and a disciple of Tolstoy and Zola, she was a shining-star amongst the thousands of immigrant women in the city of Glasgow, many of whom could neither read or write. It was she who was called upon when a neighbour had trouble at childbirth, or if good advice was being sought in matters of a domestic nature.

She had one failing, if that is the correct word: an inability to relax. She found it impossible to sit still. If not cooking, cleaning, ironing or washing, she had to knit, sew or do lacework. Her crocheting was a work of art, much of it now in the possession of my two sisters. One of my mental pictures of Mum never varies. She is sitting at a table, reading a Yiddish newspaper, and doing crochet. At the same time she has two babies (one in each arm, asleep); *all this at the same time*. In all probability this is my earliest memory, and the infants are my younger brother and sister. I would then be about 5 years of age.

I remember too being taken to school for the first time. I was, incidentally, a horrible child, bad-tempered, snivelling, ever demanding attention. What I needed (and never received) was a damned good old-fashioned thrashing from time to time. Mother would not permit my brothers to impart a slap on my face or bottom, as she abhorred any display of violence. As for Dad, he was as soft as putty. He was a gentle, kindly old man (a tailor by trade) who was happy to leave his wife in complete charge of bringing up the kids in her own way. On looking back, I now realise that corporal punishment, if administered justly and wisely, does more good than harm. Indeed, the old adage: 'spare the rod and spoil the child' has much wisdom.

Anyway, with Mum holding my hand, a shopping-bag in her other hand, I was led down South Portland Street and along Norfolk Street, to the school at the corner of Oxford Street and Buchan Street, Gorbals Primary. All along the route I was protesting tearfully. 'I don't want to go to school, Mammy. I'm frightened. I want to stay with you.'

She stopped at a corner-shop (Bain's sweet-shop). 'If I buy you sweeties, will you be a good boy, and stop crying?'

My reply brought a smile to her lips. She then realised I was no fool. I was not a Scottish-Jew for nothing. This was evident by my words.

'Well, Mammy, if you buy me sweets, *and* give me a penny to buy more after school, then I'll be good.' Talk about black-mail. What a crafty little basket I was.

Within a short time, I was placed in the care of Miss Flett, my first teacher. She was a tall, bespectacled spinster, who was very capable and well understood child psychology. She whispered something to Mum, who furtively disappeared from the scene. I had suddenly lost interest in everything except the huge, wonderful rocking-horse, on which I was placed, reins in my hands. This was fantastic for a little boy who had never seen such a toy. I was as happy as a pig in shit. I was a cowboy . . . Tom Mix, Buck Jones . . . riding over the range on the look-out for hostile Injuns. Oh! To recapture the joys and imagination of childhood! That fanciful world we return to, usually, when we become geriatrics.

It has to be remembered that Britain of the 1920s was not a land of milk and honey. To be sure, we had a great Empire – we British had conquered far and wide. What we could not take by political intrigue and threats we took by 'gun-boat diplomacy'. Who would dare defy the might of the Raj? Who would dare incur our displeasure? We were then the greatest industrial nation on earth. And yet . . . I repeat, and yet . . . our cities (at least the working-class areas) were a disgrace to any civilised land. The slums built during the Industrial Revolution soon became unfit for human habitation. In Glasgow, for instance, miles of grey tenements dominated the skyline, their chimneys belching forth smoke and grime into the already polluted atmosphere. They housed, apart from the indigenous Scottish families, Jewish immigrants from Russia and eastern Europe who had fled from the pogroms endemic to these lands; and thousands of Irish families who had likewise fled, not from murderous Jew-baiters, but from the potato famine of the 1880s. They were hard-working people too, who were glad to find employment in the building-trade, the mines, on the streets and making roads, or in the factories; Scotland was a sanctuary for the homeless, the oppressed and the victims of injustice and intolerance.

The dominant factor, in relation to poor housing conditions, lack of proper sanitation, food shortages and growing unemployment, was the fact that the country had just emerged from the horrors of the First Great War. Ex-servicemen and their families were not getting any benefits from 'the war to end all wars'. On the contrary, their fight for survival in post-war years was even grimmer than the trenches – and this is most eloquent indeed, for tens of thousands died terribly within and around those rat-infested mud-holes of Hell and Damnation.

The diseases of the time affected almost every family: tuberculosis, rickets, pneumonia. These ailments were attributed to bad housing and malnutrition. There was infestation of rats and mice, with lice, bed- and wood-bugs, cockroaches and beetles, to back up the rivers of excreta which often flowed from common lavatories situated on tenements, between floors.

So much for the land fit for heroes. This was the lot of too many nice people. First World War posters had proclaimed: 'YOUR COUNTRY NEEDS YOU'. You were exhorted to fight and die, if need be, for the glory of England. But, after doing so, the surviving poor devils were discarded like a bunch of rags. Their purpose has been served. Now, in effect, if they ask something in return from the state, they are told politely to 'piss off'. The ordinary chap is expendable.

I suppose that, comparatively speaking, we Caplans had little to complain of. For we lived at 77 South Portland Street, top flat, right, all the time from the age of 18 months until one year before the Second World War (1938) when I was a 23 year-old vigorous young man, ready for anything. That street was wide, long (leading up to the famous suspension foot-bridge) and ideal for the playing of games such as football and rounders, and the chasing of girls into the mouths of tenements (called 'closes') wherein we played at Mammies and Daddies. Many young girls lost what was then termed as their most prized possession . . . their virginity.

By today's standards, of course, our behaviour was tame indeed. To the best of my knowledge, all the young ladies who were prepared and willing to drop their bloomers were over 16 years old. Rape, as such, was almost unknown. Nor were muggings, attacks on old ladies and children, and drug addiction. And I am speaking of the so-called infamous Gorbals.

Sunday was bath-night, so my big sister Etty would be given the task of looking for my younger brother Jerry, Anna, the youngest of our family, and myself. We would be playing in our own street, or possibly with friends in Abbotsford Place, Cumberland Street, or Apsley Place. As often as not, we attempted to elude her, but to no avail. Etty had her friend Dolly Murchie to assist her in the capture of the three mavericks. As far as I was concerned, I had no objections to being collared by the lovely, delectable Dolly. She was a neat little blonde, five years my senior, and perpetually smelling of eau de cologne and cheap powder. I would be about 10 or 11 years old, and the biological urge was beginning to stir in my blood, though, truthfully, I had my first sexual intercourse at the age of 19. Up to that time, I was simply playing, or experimenting with the girls. As stated, I enjoyed other games, especially cowboys and Indians. And I was not averse to fighting with any boy who challenged me for one reason or another.

Number 77 must have been considered as 'good property' in those days. Why? Well, for a start each flat did have an inside toilet; also, each storey had only two families, that is, two to each of the three landings. Furthermore, the whole street and and most of the homes within were kept in a remarkably high state of cleanliness, owing to the fact that these were the homes of many professional people, such as doctors, dentists, teachers, rabbis and Church of Scotland ministers. Dad, as a master-tailor during the '14–'18 war, had a War Department contract for army uniforms, and so we were able to keep up with the Jones's (or should I say, the Cohens?).

How well I remember that old zinc bathtub, placed between two chairs, next to a blazing coal-fire in an open grate. The smell of coal-tar soap; the ritual of discarding our old, playing clothes (for washing next day) and the laying-out of our 'good' clothes for school next day.

At that time of my life, *circa* 1926, my older brothers and sister were then beyond the kitchen-bathing stage, and so they utilised the amenities of the nearby Gorbals Public Baths in the Main Street.

Opposite the baths stood two places of pleasure, the source of great thrills and delight for children of the area. These were the Palace Cinema, with Diamond's Dancing Academy above – both now defunct, and the Princess Theatre, still standing like an oasis of the desert as one of Glasgow's cultural attractions, but re-named the Citizens Theatre. Ours was just one branch of a large family-tree whose roots had been well established during many generations in Lithuania.

The chronology of the South Portland Street Caplans is as follows: Dad and Mum, from Vilna and Kovno, escapers from Czarist terror. Yet they, as other immigrants, would look back with much sadness and refer wistfully to that poxy, Cossack-infested country as '*der heim*' (the homeland, the old country). No doubt this was due to thoughts of loved ones, such as old parents, destined to die alone, amidst an apathetic people, of a savage regime.

The first-born child, after seven years of marriage – an arranged marriage through the good offices of a *shadchan* (matchmaker)... was Carl in 1906. Then came Samuel Robert (Sam), Etty, Louis and Jack (or as I was mis-named on my birth certificate Ezra. Mum meant it to be Israel, after her rabbinical father so I made a compromise later by labelling myself Israel Jack). Then came Gershon (Jerry) followed by Anna, making seven surviving children, almost equally spaced with 18 months between each. Two had died in infancy, otherwise there would have been nine little mouths to feed.

All of us, I believe, were born at home. In the years separating the two Great Wars women were made of sterner stuff. They were tough, dedicated to family and home, sans frills or fanciful ideas, and in the main had no time for self-pity nor hysteria. That pioneer-breed has made way for pampered and petted females who demand the best of two worlds. They want to be treated with respect and reverence; and at the same time they expect equality with men, complete emancipation, and to compete in every form of masculine activity. Already I can hear some lady readers remark – 'What a horrible, male chauvinist pig that man Caplan is.' I do not intend to offend; I merely state my innermost feelings in terms of women, past and present, based on the experiences of a long life. 'What profiteth a woman if she gains the world – and loses her femininity?'

How often one hears the expression: 'the good old days'. Sure, some things *were* good then. There was less crime, for a start. A different set of values existed, such as parental respect, and a healthy respect for law and order. Disicpline at school may have been rigid, and teachers had the authority to use the strap, if required. So what? A 14 year-old boy or girl, leaving school for the big world outside (unless academically suited for college and university), would be well-equipped to cope with the problems of work and making a living. It has been officially reckoned by educationalists that school-leavers of yesteryear (even at 14) were far more advanced in the three R's and the sciences than their counterparts of the present day who leave at 16.

On the credit side, however, and it cannot be denied, in terms of health, physical fitness, and wealth (pocket-money) the modern youngster has the best scores. Rather, I would venture to suggest, they are too damned well-off. Clothes, styles, music, and movies, are all geared for their specific market and enjoyment. And the question this poses is: do they become better adults as a result of their Utopian life-style? Well, I have many reservations on that subject.

The harshness of those living-conditions, with the special emphasis on working-class housewives having to feed, clothe and generally look after a large family, was reflected by the lower standards of living, the deprivations all around, widespread poverty, with few families ever having experienced the beneficial effects of a holiday in the country or at the sea-side.

It took skill, determination and perseverence, not to mention love and dedication, for a mother to concentrate on the welfare of her offspring. For many years, with a total income of two pounds and ten shillings, my mother had to provide all. I repeat, we were amongst the better-off families. Certainly, such things are relevant. Smokers could buy 10 fags for 4*d*. (Woodbines); a loaf of bread was 4*d*.; a pint of milk 1*d*., a bag of coal, 9*d*.; and for the rich few who had cars, petrol was 11 pence per gallon. Nevertheless, our weekly bill for provisions alone came to 25 shillings, or half of our total income. Unemployment money and social security help was practically unknown. At best, a family *might* be given two shillings weekly if, after being willing to submit to a very strict investigation into their financial position (this was called a 'Means Test') they were found to be at starvation level.

This was the background against which over-tired, work-worn mothers had to contend. Let me take you inside our old house – a glance into the past. Bear in mind, as stated, our lot was a happier one than so many others.

After climbing three sets of stairs you arrived at two doors, with name-plates. On the left were our immediate neighbours, the Guttentags. They were very religious Jews, with a *mezuzah* on its slanting position above eye-level on doorpost. This oblong metal strip contains a parchment (or rolled-up Scroll of the Law). The orthodox Jew touches his fingers to his lips, then to the *mezuzah* each time he enters or leaves his home.

No *mezuzah* on the Caplan door. Why? Because God does not require reminding that we were just as good Jews without ostentation. After all, with a name like CAPLAN clearly shown, centrally, surely visitors would realise we were not Irish. Again, all the boys are circumcised according to tradition, and we do not need to flash the penis to prove us to be nice, Jewish boys. Having said this, I am still as ever quite prepared to show any curious, doubting lady (providing she be attractive) that my credentials are in order...

I was once called a 'facetious little fucker' by a Gentile friend after he had made several observations on the difference between Jewish and non-Jewish girls. I knew he was interested in my young sister, Anna. In a sort of roundabout way, he was fishing for information about her habits, and attitude to boys. He was a poor angler. I merely led him up the garden path; he is perhaps still wondering whether there be an anatomical difference – let us say from the vertical to the horizontal – in respect of a love-making position.

So, the caller would pull the brass outer bell. On the door being opened, my Mum would speak in English. Perhaps she would say: 'Jack is not at home, but you are welcome to come in and wait for him. He won't be long.' Enter visitor. A long dark passage. First door on the right, the kitchen. Now the kitchen was, in those days, many rooms in one; for preparing and cooking food; dining room; library; lounge and bedroom. Bedroom? Yes, a recess bed (or hole-in-wall bed) was common in Scottish kitchens.

Then, assuming the visitor was given a guided tour of the manor, he would then leave the kitchen and find the WC directly opposite the front door; just a WC, no bath, no wash-hand basin, no toilet-paper, no mod-cons; if he did wish to 'spend a penny', well, yesterday's newspaper was cut neatly into 6 inch squares and nailed on to a convenient wall.

Then bedroom one, with two large double beds. Here slept Carl and

Louis in one of them; the other was for Sam, Jerry, and me: all five boys in one room.

Finally, there was what we called the 'big room' – really the largest room of all, being the only front room with a view of the street. Herein slept the two girls, Etty and Anna. Mum and Dad slept in the recess bed in the kitchen.

That big room, apart from being the girls' bedroom, was our *pièce de résistance*. Sometimes referred to as the 'parlour', or the 'sitting-room' (we all have at times illusions of grandeur), it was indeed our pride and joy. It was large, square, sunny, and adorned with pictures of the Russian novelist Leo Tolstoy and his French counterpart Emile Zola, giving an air of dignity and an atmosphere of appreciation of the arts, specifically literature. That room, furthermore, contained the violin, diplomas and medals which belonged to brother Carl. He had been the brightest pupil at the Athenaeum, the Glasgow School of Music. A large piano alongside one wall, with reams of music-sheets (for violin and piano) completed the decor. Incidently, brother Louis was then taking lessons on the pianoforte.

I do not know how, or why, our 'big room' was the largest room in the whole of South Portland Street. Not being a builder, nor an architect, I can only hazard a guess. During construction in the mid-nineteenth century, it was apparent that our street had been better planned, with better material used and more care taken. The fact of *all* homes in the street having inside WCs was in itself evidence that the planners had earmarked the property as being for professional occupants as opposed to the 'working-man'. Talk about class distinction, snobbery, it makes one bloody sick to think about it. But whatever, for some reason best known to the contractors, our front room owed its extra space to the fact of it being 'pinched' from our neighbour. His loss was our gain. Funnily, this was never explained to us, nor did our neighbour ever question the matter.

I do know that when a marriage, or a circumcision, or any other outstanding function took place – including meetings and large birthday parties – our big room was the venue. I remain convinced to this day that the Caplans of South Portland Street, were better known than the Barretts of Wimpole Street.

Mum would offer the visitor, any visitor, a cup of tea, always with a piece of cake, or biscuit, or sandwich. She was always kindly and generous to the extreme. On opening the door for me, mother would then speak in rapid Yiddish. Where have I been? Was I OK? There is someone to see you. The poor boy has been waiting, so patiently. Then, as always, a big kiss in welcome. Yes, that was my 'maw'.

Mum was always thrifty, and able to stretch pennies to shillings; once she proudly opened an old tea-caddy (then utilised as a savings-bank) and showed us the amount then accumulated: an unbelievable total of *ten pounds*. This was a princely sum in the year of our Lord, 1926. We were astounded at this wealth. She was saving for shoes (needed badly by Jerry and me; kids playing football in the streets quickly go through footwear) and linoleum for the kitchen and hall. Carpets were almost an unknown luxury.

From childhood to manhood Jerry and I wore hand-knitted socks, jerseys, and on occasion underwear, all made by Mother. We were always dressed alike, and though I was older by eighteen months, few people could remember who was who. Many took us for twins. Yet we were really quite different. Although Jerry was of the same height, he was much fairer than I, with very attractive blue eyes, he was slighter of build, and had a much sweeter disposition. He was much more liked and justly so. With black hair, and moods to match, for I was more capricious, my blue-grey eyes mirrored the sullen nature and restlessness which ever simmered within.

Sam and I were the hawks, Louis and Gershon the doves. As for Carl, he was volcanic. Highly-strung and neurotic, he was an exceedingly intelligent fellow noted for his intolerance and aggressive manners.

Mother was a small, plump lady, more Russian-looking than Jewish. Her jet-black thin hair was pulled back with a bun at the end. I suppose this could be described as a severe hair-style, but it was quite common among the women of Eastern Europe. She wore, always, hand-knitted cardigans and black woollen stockings. Her shoes were brogues; never at any time had she worn elegant or high-heeled shoes. She never used make-up or jewellery, apart from her gold wedding ring. In later years she suffered badly from varicose veins on her legs, which contributed to her death at the age of 82.

Some 15 years prior to her death she was admitted to hospital. Severe pain in one leg necessitated her admission. After a few days of tests and observation, the surgeon approached her bed. Gravely, he said:

'Mrs Caplan, I have some bad news for you. As you know, we have given your case careful attention. My colleagues and I, after much consideration have arrived at a decision. The only thing which can save your life is for us to amputate your left leg.'

Mother, naturally, was shocked by this blow. Outwardly, and typically, she showed no alarm. After a few moments which allowed her to gather her thoughts, she replied in a quiet, even voice:

'I want to take this opportunity of thanking you, Mr . . . , and all the doctors and nurses here who have shown so much kindness to me. But I can only give you one answer. You will take my leg off on one condition. This being that *you cut off my head at the same time.*'

The following day Carl and Etty called at the hospital to take her home, by taxi. She showed no concern for her own situation, or for the throbbing pain. The first question, to Etty, was:

'Zog meer, mine keend, voss marcht der keender? OI-VEY! Der orramer keender!' ('Tell me, my child, how are the children? Woe is me! The poor children.')

They cried. We at home wept. And Mum, her first remark on arrival at home:

'Forgive me children for neglecting you so. But don't worry . . . Mammy's home now. I'll soon have a nice meal ready for you . . .'

And she soldiered on for another 15 years before she finally died. Is it any wonder I am near to tears when I hear the words of *My Yiddishy Mama*?

Dad

Dad was a quiet, unobtrusive man. Five feet, 10 inches tall, handsome, moustached and very hard-working. He became an apprentice tailor at the age of 10 or 11. He was not sure of his age as, apparently, no records of births and deaths took place in his village (hamlet) of Lithuania. I reckoned this was due to the attitudes of officials. Who cared whether Jews lived or died? So unimportant! For sure, they would say: 'All things have a purpose. Jews are born to provide fun for the peasants who get bored and drunk. Then we can invade their villages, burn them out, rape their women – and kill any Jew-boy who wants to be a hero.'

I never discovered details of my father's method of escape from his home-land. Why he and others wished to flee was obvious to the world. He did not have mother's shrewdness, nor her education, and lacked the family support given to mother by her parents. More important, he could only speak Yiddish and thus was at a great disadvantage in terms of communicating with Russian travel-agents and officials. I would therefore assume his arrival in England was a great achievement.

The fact was, that he made the journey; shabby and penniless, he had to look up addresses of kinsfolk in English towns; he had been robbed by con-men on board the ship, for Dad was a simple, trusting person, one might say, naive. The brotherhood of international Jewry was, and still is, established in all large centres of Jewish concentration – I do not like the word 'Ghetto'. He received from one of those organisations, the Board of Guardians, food, clothing, a little money to tide him over the worst first weeks, and the address of a family who would provide a room and warmth. With moral backing and further support from his relatives, he soon found a job in the tailoring trade. By the time a local *shatran* was commissioned to find a suitable wife for him, he was settled and orientated to the British way of life.

Dad was a comedian – but unaware of it. Well do I recall the ecstasy, and the shame, when on about two occasions each year during the summer he would take Jerry, Anna and me out for the day to one of the many beautiful villages around Glasgow. We went by tram-car, the cheapest means of travel. A penny fare took us a mile and 2½d (maximum fare) would take us approximately 20 miles in any direction. We could go to such places as the towns of Paisley, Barrhead, Airdrie, to villages like Kilbarchan, Millerston, Clarkston, and so on. Oh what joy! First he would give each of us a whole penny (for ice-cream at the terminus). And he let us climb to the top deck of the car, with a much better view of the route, this being usually reserved for smokers. Then would come the bitter pill, or as Jerry had termed it, our price for the outing. We made for the top front of the vehicle, as this provided the best all-round view. The wooden seats were quite comfortable. As the conductor appeared, with the usual cry of 'Fares please!' Dad would grin widely, and shout to him:

'Hullo Johnny! Dese are my tree cheeldrin . . . ' (then came the embarrassment which always petrified us) . . . 'Di big boy' (pointing to me) 'is Cox. Dat udder boy iss Chox, and di vee gerl, my leetle babykins, is Box.'

Jack, Jerry and Anna (*always* on a tram-car, and do not ask me why) became Cox, Chox and Box. But more was to come, alas! For this opening chorus was just the overture.

'Look, Johnny, I vant vun ticket, dat's for me, to vare you're goin'. You understand? vun ticket for me – for I'm de man. OK! Vell . . . for di cheeldren I van tree halfs . . . ' We knew what was to follow, so we bent our heads to hide the blushes . . . ' remember, *not* di *halfs* of visky . . . no, no, for dat's for drinking (you like visky, Johnny?)'

The good nature and humour of most Scotsmen never failed to appreciate the situation, (an immigrant father taking his kids out for a run to the country) and they at all times were friendly. The conductor would smile, give us a pat on the head, and say something about 'nice looking kids'. Dad seldom failed to offer the man to retain the change, in lieu of a drink, for like mother, he was generous. I have never known any conductor to accept a tip, to their credit.

Dad may not have been endowed with a surplus of brain-matter, but he was no fool. He was a first-class tradesman. I remember it was he himself who put it most aptly one day when mother had scolded him for commencing work at home on a customer's suit. She had rebuked him for drinking a bit too much beforehand. Dad was fond of whisky, but normally only drank on an evening when work was done. This particular occasion was on a Sunday, and after dinner he had reduced a full bottle of the golden liquid by almost half. He turned to her, his blue eyes ablaze with anger, and said:

'Fanny, do you think I'm a *meshuginer* (madman)? Let me tell you dis much... a good doctor cuts up bodies to make people well. I'm a *shneider* (tailor) and I cut up cloth, and ven I'm finished, a customer also feels vell. Vell-dressed. So you must trust me, Faigele.' (This was Mum's name in Yiddish.)

Dad, in his own way, possessed a unique brand of philosophy which belied his outward simplicity. He was to a certain extent an enigma. I will cite two situations in which he was involved, and from which he extricated himself with remarkable ease:

His favourite pub, the Club bar, in Oxford Street, Gorbals, was where he liked to spend an evening with friends. There he played the only game he knew, dominoes. One night of winter, with howling winds blowing and heavy rain lashing the streets, he arrived cold and wet at the Club, went straight to the bar as usual, and was given his usual drink by the bar man, 'Johnny'. Nearly all of Dad's acquaintances were called 'Johnny', this being much easier than having to remember every man's christian name. He had just paid for the whisky when the door blew open, and a huge Irishman staggered into the establishment. He was a casual customer and a known trouble-maker. Paddy made for Dad, who happened to be the only customer standing at the bar counter, awaiting his change.

'To be sure, it's a hell of a night. Will yi buy me a drink, Jew-boy?'

Dad looked hard at the man, already the worse of drink, unsteady and menacing. The barman prudently kept his silence, and distance. Even though my father was a regular and popular customer, discretion was often the best part of valour (so it is said).

'In the first place,' said my old man, 'I don't know you... in the second place, I don't vant to know you...'

Then in that well-known Jewish intonation, with the words rising and lowering, and drawn out for full emphasis, he continued: 'If I vas a younger man I vould trow my visky at you, b-u-t dat vould be a vaste of good visky. So-o . . . I tell you vat I vill do. I vill give you a game of dominoes, and if *you* vin . . . vell, den I buy you a drink. If *I* vin, den you vill go to hell away from here, yes?'

A long silence prevailed. The atmosphere was electric. Men fidgeted nervously at the tables. At any moment hell would break loose, and poor Morris (my Dad) would be battered at the first onslaught. Verily, the scene was reminiscent of a Hollywood drama. Then came the anti-climax. Paddy (or was he Mick? He was no Johnny) glowered with disbelief, his open mouth making him look even more stupid, and was heard to say:

'Bejasis! I don' want to play you bloody dominoes. Sure! That's a game for bloody Jews and Proddies' (Protestants).

And with that he turned around, walked to the door, again turned, then shouted at Dad:

'Oill be back. Just you wait and see. And Oi'll have some of my friends wi' me. We know how to deal with "hard" men like you.'

That incident became legend. Men were to talk of it for many years to come. What brought tears of laughter to many eyes was the Irishman's misinterpretation of Dad's words. He took it as defiance, a challenge to bring about ridicule, or a veiled threat to stall him until Dad's friends would make a concerted attack on the intruder. Nothing could be funnier. My dad a 'hard' man? The poor man simply wanted to placate the fellow. To maintain the peace. To avoid conflict. He wanted to go back home in one piece – but not at the price of buying a drink for a bully and coward. *That was my Dad.*

The other incident involved brother Sam. It was 1930. Sam was then aged 22. Like Dad, he was fond of whisky. He was much closer to his father than the rest of us, for he was then working alongside the old man in a tailoring factory (a job he despised) and was mixing in bad company. As a matter of fact, Sam was the considered leader of a really tough bunch whose territory was based at Coburg Street, almost opposite the Club bar. He was feared as much by the family (owing to a vicious temper) as he was by the young men of the district. His reputation was earned the hard way. Being handsome, more Italian-looking than Jewish, his swarthy appearance and broad shoulders captivated the girls . . . and he loved the ladies. While standing at the corner with some of the boys, a tall, well-built, red-haired man approached them, and said:

'I'm looking for a cunt called Caplan.'

Sam spoke up: 'I'm *Mr* Caplan, Ginger, and if you ever call me a dirty name again I'll sweep the street with your guts.'

Ginger then explained that Sam had taken away his girl, who claimed to be pregnant. Sam admitted he was having an affair with the female in question, and added:

'She came to me because *you're* useless. You might be carrying a baton on the side of your pants, but you've got nothing between your legs.'

For Sam was observant. The man was evidently a police officer, off duty. His trousers were blue – what was called police-blue and the outline of his truncheon was evident.

Angry words were bandied back and forward. The inevitable outcome came. It was agreed to have 'a square-go'. This meant a fight between the two belligerents, without interference from anyone. This was an accepted code of conduct amongst warring factions in Glasgow, a sort of 'gentlemen's agreement' which was *never* dishonoured. And that is what happened. They all went into the nearest back-court, a circle was formed, the contestants stripped to the waist, then faced each other. No referee, no rules regarding ethics, no time limits were imposed – certainly Queensbury rules were scoffed at. It was always just two men, bare-fisted in a fight to a finish. One had to win, one to lose. If the stranger won, gangland etiquette allowed him to walk away unmolested. For he would have won, also, the respect of those who were spectators. If the man representing the 'home' team won, then his reputation would soar to ever-increasing heights. He would be uncrowned king . . . a hero . . . an idol.

That fight turned out to be the fight of the century. Sam was living it up. Wine, whisky and women. He was having his fill of all. And so he was flabby, soft in the wrong places, and short of stamina. Conversely, the young copper was well-muscled, very fit, and well motivated. *He* was fighting for a young girl's honour, and the honour of the police-force. Furthermore, being a Highlander (a *choorta*) he had little regard for the Lowland Scots. Yes, funny again. His opponent was a little Jewish chap of the Gorbals, and a full six inches shorter, not to mention the disadvantage of being some three stones lighter.

Bill Riffkind, a close friend of Sam's, later told me of the fight. His running commentary was oft-repeated, I guess. Sam realised his adversary had most in his favour; in previous such fights, he would have attacked at once with fists and boots, but this brave man-mountain was no pushover. This fight required initially the use of brain. The brawn was tipped in favour of the cop. The landing of one blow from such ham-fists would mean a smashed face. David and Goliath indeed. And tactics had to vary. Sam adopted the style of the recent American world-champion, Mohammed Ali (unknown, of course, then). He used his feet, danced, parried, and refused to mix blow for blow. Benny Caplan was a well-known London boxer of that period, and several of Sam's pals, in fact, had called him 'Benny'. Within the first three minutes both men were sweating profusely, and no blood was spilled. The impression Bill had was agonising. Sam was about to be toppled from his 'throne'. Of the two, he was faring worse, panting, gasping, even appearing to be near collapse. And then it happened, the miracle of miracles, comparable to the opening of the Red Sea for the Children of Israel. The young copper rushed bull-like at Sam, swung a terrific right which landed above the head, just displacing a lot of air; lost his balance, fell to the ground – and as he rolled over quickly to make a scramble to his feet, Sam pounced with his booted feet. Three mighty kicks on the ribs and it was all over.

It was closing-time at the Club bar, a week later. Dad was leaving with a friend. As they arrived at the corner, four men walked up to them, and one pointed at Dad.

'That's his old man.'

'Where's your son, Sam?' demanded one of them.

'Vot do you vant with my Sam?'

'That's not *your* business!'

'Look, if you have anything against my boy, den it *is* my business. If you don't go avay, I will call the police.'

The tallest of the group then spoke: 'If you report this to the police, *you'll* be in trouble! Maybe we'll give you a wee sample of what your bastard son is going to get.'

Dad blazed with anger. 'My son may be vild, but he's not a bastard. Another ting, he's not a coward... he's a better man than any of you scum.' A pause. 'Nu? if you vant to fight somebody, den hit *me*. Den you vill vin, and go home like heroes to your vives and cheeldren. Vill that make you feel better?'

Whether that made them feel better, one will never know. But as Mr Harris (Dad's friend) said later: 'It was amazing! They looked at each other and gave a shrug of their shoulders, then the big man said to Morris: 'Your son is a lucky man, having you for a father. You're a fine old chap.'. Then they walked away, humbled and dejected. Possibly ashamed too.

Dad died one year before the Second World War, 1938. We were glad he had not lived to see four of his sons in Army and Air Force uniform. For this surely would have broken his heart – he loved us so much.

Brother Carl

To Carl we owe so much. He became 'clan' chief after father's death, yet for most of his life, even when only a boy, he was Mum's adviser and confidant. He was exceedingly brilliant, hard-working and a genius. He had been born with a photographic memory and an unlimited store for knowledge, and the capacity to gather and keep information on any subject under the sun. He knew about religion, politics, philosophy, astrology, music, and numerous other facts and figures relating to human endeavour. He was the nearest possible to being a walking encyclopedia. Uncanny, perhaps, but absolutely true.

But the price he had to pay was far too much. It can be said he was a victim of circumstances. Let me elucidate.

I have already mentioned that Carl was born seven years after the marriage of our parents. Those years until his birth as a bouncing, healthy six-pounder, were full of grief, especially for Mum. For large families then was the in-thing, the norm; no woman can graciously accept being barren. Besides this, Mother was lonely and lacked companionship. To be sure, she now had two sisters in Glasgow, Sophie and Mary. Sophie was married to an eccentric Regular soldier, and lived in the east-end of the city, whilst Mary, being a child of school-age, was being brought up as a daughter. But this factor did not fill the aching gap, the longing, the heart-yearning, in her maternal breast.

Dad, with all due respect, was not exactly the most suitable husband. Compatibility did not exist. (The matchmaker must have been a cowboy.) In the first place, they had been brought up in different environments. Her background was middle-class, cultured, my maternal grandfather being a rabbi. He had been a man of standing in his community, a sage, a pillar of his society, a learned man. (He was murdered by Cossacks during a pogrom.) Dad, on the other hand, was a product of the struggling, poverty-ridden uneducated Ghetto members. They survived by clinging to tradition, and to each other. Hundreds of villages containing oppressed Jews were similar to Anatevka (which featured in the wonderful movie *Fiddler on the Roof*). Dad was a work-horse. He provided for us the necessities of life – food, shelter, clothing. Mother and the children however saw little of him. For when his job finished at night, he would make for his favourite pub(s) and spend the whole evening with his cronies, drinking, playing dominoes, and talking of the 'old days' in that far-off land of persecution and misery. He could never grasp the essentials, the requirements, the obligations of living in a western society. The matter of paying rent, rates, bills of any sort, or taking a child to dentist or doctor, or when need be, to the school in order to enquire into the progress (or otherwise) of his offspring were not part of his world. All this he left to Mother.

I suppose it can be said, on his behalf, that he was aware of his poor and very limited English. And every day was a working day. Never-theless, whilst he doted on his children, he had no interest in their studies, hobbies, friends, or pursuits. This was Mother's domain. His passion for work was insatiable, an admirable quality in a man. But as for all things in life, moderation is the key-word. There must be a time and place for everything. No woman should be expected to bring up a large family on her own. It's just not cricket.

If ever a baby brought tremendous joy and fulfilment to a home, turned a darkness into light and a longing into glorious reality, that baby was Carl. As with his following brothers and sisters, the confinement was at home. Usually a midwife was present . . . if not, Mother knew the drill. There was no hospital ward, no smell of carbolic or disinfectant, no bouquet of flowers, get well cards, or baskets of fruit, just lots and lots of love awaiting the newcomer. A spank on the bottom never failed to produce its first howl of protest, then the cleansing process took place, and the 'miracle' was wrapped inside a cosy, warm blanket – then it was placed next to Mother for the first looks of adoration and wonder.

Carl, by no stretch of the imagination, could ever be called good-looking. Try telling this to any mother. From the moment of her first touch, that little bundle became her main reason for living. He was the apple of her eye, the salt of her earth, the source of her strength – her everything. And so it came to pass. My big brother Carl became the most utterly-spoiled and pampered child of all. Whilst my parents undoubtedly loved all their children, and would vehemently deny showing favouritism towards one in particular . . . *all of us knew better.*

Perhaps the only member of the family who at times showed resentment was Sam, the next in line. He later became my protector, my minder, *the* brother who claimed that I, and I alone, was from the same mould. True, we were the two boys who did stand out from the other three by temper and temperament. Both of us caused Mother no end of anxiety and trouble. We were the cause of dissension at home, the culprits involved in street brawls, the local tough-guys. Yet never did we instigate a fracas; provocation always came from the other fellows, for various reasons; maybe they didn't like Jews, or as often happened, they simply threw a challenge in order to test our ability to rule the roost. Some have said Jews were clever with money, but useless as fighters. How little they knew. The Israelites were a warrior-race long before the Romans came to Europe to control the barbarians; a handful of Jewish men, women and children held a whole legion of Roman troops at bay for many months at a place called Massada. Remember the fighting qualities of the Maccabeans; think of the Warsaw ghetto and the amazing resistance therein of a few ordinary men and women who fought a whole battalion of Nazi storm-troopers, while Polish people stood by and wondered at such bravery. I could go on, and on. But this book is not meant to be a history of Jewish conquest, only a true story, in brief, of one family, in the Gorbals of Glasgow between the two World Wars.

Sam's resentment was, in all fairness, not without a certain justification. Carl could do no wrong in the eyes of his parents, and he was not slow in taking advantage of this situation. Though Sam was the younger of the two, he was not afraid of giving Carl a hard kick on the *tochas* (arse) if he had stepped out of line. Carl would scream hysterically, like a castrated pig, out of proportion to a mere arse-kick. At this point I have to say he was, from an early age, exceedingly theatrical. He would have made a great dramatic actor. Both Mum and Dad would however immediately assume that 'poor Ca-raly' was the innocent victim of his hooligan brother. Sam was ever-labelled as the *baitz* (ruffian). Sam was scolded . . . Carl commiserated with promises of sweets for being 'injured'. This, in truth, was the back-cloth to most dramas in our household.

This was only a part of the cause of friction. For blind love, like blind hate, can be fatal. Too much was expected from Carl. Mother took him for lessons on the violin when he was five years old. He excelled in this, and was to become, in later years, a teacher of that instrument, and a member of a cinema orchestra (before the talkies were invented).

On leaving school, he went into Dad's factory and trained as a machinist. For a while he worked aboard Cunard liners as a musician, plying between Glasgow and Canadian ports. In my humble opinion, no person of tender years should be burdened with a constant concentration of learning and training, unless interspersed with lots of leisure-time and outdoor pursuits. Carl had no time for these, or possibly our parents failed him by not encouraging him in that direction. This I do not know.

It can be said Carl had developed a parochial outlook by virtue of his own mastery over all his school studies, the violin, and his trade.This can be assessed by his utter contempt of all people who possessed no academic qualifications. In other words, he was guilty of gross snobbery. This would appear to be paradoxical – yet it was so.

That attitude rose to a crescendo when, at the age of 19, or was it 20? he found himself in a dilemma. Indeed, the whole country was thrown out of gear. A catastrophe occurred: The General Strike of 1926. I was then eleven years of age. Caught between strike and slump, the tailoring trade ground to a halt. If people had money (and few did) there was no one left to produce their suits or costumes. By the same token, cinemas had no operators, and so few halls remained open. An impasse had been reached. In effect, Carl (as thousands of others) was out of work, and at a dead-end.

Carl however was too active mentally to take this lying down. He had an idea, then went into conference with Mother. His plan was endorsed; he then sat down and wrote a letter to the Director of Education in Bath Street; and that gentleman's reply was positive. Carl was about to enter a new career – as a school-teacher. For four long, weary years he studied. The strike had ended soon after he had commenced this venture so he was again at work during the day, as a machinist, but after getting home at 6 p.m. and hastily eating a meal, he went into his (or should I say, the communal) bedroom, and worked long into the night.

Well do I recall going to bed, and watching him pore over books under candle-light. He often fell asleep across the small table in the early hours of the morning. What a man! I always admired him for his tenacity of purpose and dedication – and envied his super brain-power.

Just give this a thought. After a long night of much study and little real sleep, he had to partake of breakfast with little appetite, really too tired to eat. Then off he went to work in the factory till 6 p.m. once more. The most carefully designed machine in the world will seize up if over worked. The human brain is no exception. I put this down as a reason for brother Carl's behaviour and shortcomings; his tantrums, his many displays of neurosis, his lack of tolerance with others, and his need for understanding – which we, his brothers and sisters, failed to give. As I have said, he was a victim of circumstances, and of a strong concentration of parental love.

Carl emerged as a fully-qualified schoolteacher, MA (Hons), after four years. Shortly after he became a primary school headmaster. This was no mean achievement for the son of immigrant parents, and for a man who had left school five years before going back to college. Furthermore, he became a teacher of public-speaking, and a celebrity in that field. *Carl, I salute you!*

As I write these words, Carl is living in a Home for the aged. He is suffering from senile dementia: the deterioration of a super brain.

Sam

Sam was dark, handsome, with a smile which at best was sardonic. He was small of stature but built like a miniature tank. His body was hairy, muscled, well-shaped, and when I saw him strip for bed he reminded me of a gorilla about to pounce upon its prey. I hated having him as a bed-mate. Jerry slept at the wall-end, with me in the centre, while Sam occupied the end which was next to the other bed. At all times he slept in the nude. Not only was this unhygienic but it was most uncomfortable for me, being in close proximity to him. For he often smelled of scent and powder which had been transferred to him from one or other of his dolly-birds. To make matters worse, he always enquired if I was asleep or not. Come to think of it what can be more Irish?

More often than not, if I were awake I would not answer and feigned sleep. Any response from me would have resulted in my being kissed on the forehead and my hair tousled (and no boy is happy in being so treated, especially by a brother). He would then wax sentimental. What a complex character! Hard, wild, self-indulgent, restless, and mean. Yet with me, and only me, he showed other qualities, like tenderness, true brotherly love, genuine affection. Then would come a torrent of pet names, an avalanche of patronage:

'How is my little Eetzky today? Has my wee china been a good boy? You're the best kid in the world! Listen, Yankel (Jack) I want you to do something for me – as soon as you can . . . maybe tomorrow, eh? Tell you what it is. I was in Helen Blair's house tonight . . . couldn't do a thing to her, because her fuckin' wee brother (about your age) would not piss off.

Now he's too young for me to hit – but you can get 'im at school, or somewhere. Do that for me, and I'll give you a tanner (all to yourself). OK?'

That was a tempting offer. But in the morning, after sleeping on those terms of the 'contract', I decided to have no part of it. And to my surprise Sam said he had forgotten all about it. Either he did not wish me to get into trouble or, more probable, he did not relish the thought of giving me so much gelt – sixpence.

The Gorbals of old could be compared with parts of Stepney and Whitechapel, or the Bowery and Bronx of New York City. Many of the kids were wild, insolent and tough. Little 'Fontainroys' (children of the 'best' people) would not mix – or had to be carefully guarded.

Sam was the 'kingpin' and had every possible racket nicely tied-up. He ruled the streets in his territory like a budding Al Capone. I would say that between the ages of 12 and 25, he was the big-shot.

When he was about 12 he managed to acquire a pair of roller-skates. I guess they may have fallen off a lorry? Anyway, as most of the kids were from poor families, such a toy was a great attraction, so Sam went into the 'hiring' business. For one skate, on loan, to go round the block (a distance of perhaps 500 yards) the cost was one penny; for two skates, two pennies; any kid who took longer than 10 minutes (thus being under suspicion of going further) would be fined another two pence – or punched on the nose.

This developed into a thriving business. It was now time for expansion. By delegating 'agents' (his brothers, except Carl) to search the markets, such as 'the barrows' in the east-end, 'Paddy's' (near Clyde Street) and a few smaller ones in the south-side, two more pairs of skates were found. After cleaning and oiling, those too were ready for hiring. Revenue soared . . . business boomed. Sam's business acumen, now even more sharpened, concentrated on further expansion (Imperial Chemicals, take warning – a take-over is on the way). He returned to the markets, bought six old bicycles and renovated them, and now these too were for hire – at higher prices, of course. There was no stopping him. Looking back on those years between the two wars, and knowing Sam as I did, I am convinced that, had my parents landed in America, as intended, then he would have been in the prohibition racket, without any doubts. He would have been supplying booze to restaurants and night-clubs. Demand and supply are intertwined.

Another anecdote on my brother's wheelings and dealings, which struck me as really funny and proves that his initiative respected no boundaries. A young man from Canada was on holiday in Scotland, (I understand he was living with an aunt, locally), and had attached himself to Sam. The year was 1924. I suppose he and Sam were about the same age, 15 or 16.

Young Elmer was well-supplied with pocket-money, wore nice, expensive clothes, and had a nice accent – a sort of Yankee drawl. He wore powerful glasses and had a large wart at the side of his large nose. He was a pleasant enough lad, but ever bored. He had been Sam's best customer during his vacation, had spent a few pounds on skates and cycles, and had in fact hired these for days at a time. But apparently Elmer wanted more from life. There was something else on his mind that hot summer evening after tea.

Sam greeted him cheerfully: 'Hullo, El! What's it to be tonight . . . bike or skates?'

Elmer took off his glasses to wipe them. Maybe he was sweating, or nervous, or wondering how to broach the subject.

'No Sam! Not tonight. I want something else. I *need* something else.'

'Well, just tell your Uncle Sam what that is.'

Poor Elmer now became visibly uncomfortable, for I was nearby in my 'official' capacity as checker. The Canadian boy pointed at me. 'Tell him to fuck off. I don't want anyone to know my business.' Sam looked at me, then at Elmer. I recognised the danger sign . . . a sort of snarl camouflaged as a smile.

'That's my wee brother. We share secrets. He works here with me. *He stays!*'

Elmer was no fool. He got the message. In a voice so quiet, (I almost missed his words) he spoke.

'Do you wet the bed, Sam?'

'Yes . . . sometimes when I piss myself.'

'No, no, not *that* kind of wetness. I mean, when you think of a girl . . . when you dream of making love . . .'

'Ah! I'm with you. A *wet* dream. So you fuck the sheets?'

Elmer reddened. I too was somewhat embarrassed. But Sam was enjoying himself.

'Now, my friend. What are you wanting me to do about it?' Sam was way ahead of him. He knew exactly what the chap wanted – and *whom*. Elmer plucked up enough courage, and went on: 'That lovely girl you're walking-out with . . . the red-head. I was wondering . . . has she a friend,

or maybe a sister? Gee! what a swell gal she is. I only want someone to go
out with me . . . to the park, or the movies. I'm lonely, Sam.'

Poor bugger, I thought. An unhappy rich boy. Sex-appeal is a
commodity one cannot buy. Sam placed an arm around his shoulder,
and spoke in a soothing voice. Another sign. He had something up his
sleeve . . . an idea had germinated and was already going into action.

'You understand Yiddish, Elmer? - yes or no?'

'Just a few words. My parents were born in Canada.'

'OK! That's fair enough. You're a smart guy, Elmer, but I'm going to
make you even smarter - you'll learn quick. By tomorrow night, you'll
be a man.'

'I'm a man already. My *Barmitzvah* took place nearly three years ago.'

'So you're a man! But have you ever had your nookie?'

'Nookie? What's that?'

'Christ almighty! A "pump"! A "ride". A fuck!'

'You mean sexual intercourse? Never!'

Sammy looked at me, smiled, and said - 'Yeetzky, we've got a right
timtum here. A *yold*.' Then turning to Elmer again: 'Your *shmeckle*
(penis) tells you that it has another function - apart from pissing. How
does it tell you? Through your wet-dreams. Your bladder holds your
water, but your balls contain that lovely, sticky stuff which you waste by
spreading it all over your bed. Are you with me?'

A large smile took over the small face of Elmer. He was now beaming.
'You're wonderful, Sam. How do you know so much?'

'Never mind that! I'm going to see a wee lassie tonight; maybe she's
not as pretty as Helen, but after I have a word with her, then maybe, just
maybe, she'll let you put that cock of yours into action. And don't
worry. She'll show you how. But of course, Elmer old son, it will cost
you two pounds.'

And so it was. The following evening Sam introduced the young fellow
to a 'lady' who lived in Coburg Street. And it came to pass (as most
things do) that Elmer lost his virginity in the kitchen of a Glasgow flat.
Sam had earned thirty shillings. The 'lady' made ten bob. Everyone
concerned was happy. But by far the happiest was the young boy from
Canada.

The essential difference between Sam and me was the fact that I took life
seriously. I had more than a casual interest in politics. Whilst he was
chasing girls (or were the girls chasing him?) and always looking for an

easy pound or two, I was deeply concerned by the deteriorating political situation. The *momzer* (bastard) Hitler came to power in 1933. I had no confidence in the Prime Minister of the time – a *yold* called Chamberlain. *Yold* means 'fool' or 'simpleton'. He was that. He was politically naive too. But I shall get back to Sam. He holds the stage. He is the star of the moment.

Sammy (Sam) was unhappy at work. He had always felt that tailoring was a job more suited to women than to men. This was a silly notion, but nevertheless, that was why he genuinely believed himself to be a failure. He thought he had missed his vocation and indeed he had. Sam would have made a perfect lawyer. Sharp, witty, intelligent, persuasive, a pungent speaker, he could present a case with passion. At the turn of a switch, an emotional tirade could become jocular chit-chat. Anger to laughter. Laughter to tears. He had that magic quality. A hostile audience would, in minutes, change into one of sympathy and co-operation. This was all done by his choice of words and tone of voice. Believe me, I am presenting a true picture of Sam. And I knew him better than anyone.

In 1925 Sam decided to go to America, that *goldeneh medina* (country of gold). He was 18, fed up with everything Scotland had to offer, and hoped for a fresh start in the USA. Mother had two brothers in the States, Max in Detroit, Hyman in Chicago. Sam chose to visit Max, first and foremost, as he was Mum's younger brother, and her favourite. Max owned a large store, and a large family. A great welcome awaited his Scottish nephew.

Before leaving home, he had promised to send me a dollar note. I was over the moon at the thought of showing my pals and class-mates a real American dollar. At the time it was worth five shillings, no mean sum for a Gorbals kid, but had this promise been honoured I would not have parted with the note. It would be another link of the chain which bound Sam and me together. How proud I would be! I'd tell the world: 'My big brother Sam sent me this. And when he makes his fortune' (which was a foregone conclusion) 'then he will send me much more. And later a travel ticket – to spend a holiday with him.' Dreams, dreams, dreams. I reckon most little boys believe that their favourite big brother can conquer the world and can do no wrong. He is your protector, and bringer of comfort. *He is a God*! And though far gone, in a distant land, he is yet with you.

On the seas and far away,
On stormy seas and far away;
Nightly dreams and thoughts by day,
Are aye with him that's far away.

Robert Burns

Alas! Sam's American adventure failed. He blew it! Uncle Max treated him as a son, as did his wife and large family. He was given a job in the store, with the promise of speedy promotion to management within six months. But his restless spirit renegued. He became bored. This is hard to understand, for he had everything going for him. Knowing his temperament, of course, then anything could have happened. Sam could turn a family disagreement into a war, a difference of opinion into a drama.

He packed his belongings, made his goodbyes, and parted from his hosts. They had been so kind towards him, so very fond of the prodigal young man. Sam had never written to me, personally, but Mother received a total of four letters. In one of them a short note to me was enclosed. It read:

'Dear Eetzky, my best wee pal, Ma will tell you what I'm doing and where I'm going. America is a big country, with lots of opportunities. It's hard to explain to you...you're too young to understand, yet – but I am searching for El Dorado. (Ask Carl or Louis for the meaning of this.)
    I don't have to tell you, but for you I have a special place in my heart.
All my love,
Your big brother Sam.

I cried on reading that, quietly, in a dark corner of our hall. I felt so forlorn. So alone; so sad. The void in my life would remain during Sam's absence. If anything happened to him, my world would end.

In each of his letters he had told Mum that he was making great progress. The first two had come from Detroit. He was working for Uncle Max, and earning good money too. Then his second epistle informed us of his leaving the home of the Goldbergs, and finding a really good job with General Motors of Detroit. Doing what? He did not say. He was always progressing, money-wise. This was to be construed as a 'feather in his cap'...a rise up the ladder of success.

A third letter, some nine months after he had left home in Glasgow, told of him having joined a cargo ship as an ordinary seaman. It told of his trouble with a crew-member as the ship neared the South American port at Colombia. A fight had taken place with the Jew-hating Italian who, armed with a wrench, had tried to kill him. Sam seriously injured the fellow, and was then compelled to jump ship. He found another vessel whose captain (a Scot) was prepared to sign him on for the voyage to New York. But the 'big apple' had no appeal to Sam, although he got a temporary job in the 'rag trade'. His fourth and final letter was a distressing one. He was broke, stranded, and penniless, and pleaded with Mum to send him his return fare money.

If I had been older and wiser at the time, then I would have been sorely tempted to write back (on Mother's behalf) something like this: 'My dear son, I must regretfully inform you, not with malice but with sorrow, that money is not easy to come by. To remind you, it was I who scraped together your passage-money in the first instance. At great sacrifice. I can only suggest that the feathers you had gained for your hat, or your head, during your 10 months in America, should be collected then stuck up your *tochas*. Then you can fly home.'

But Mum was Mum. She cried for hours, heart-broken. Her poor boy, alone and hungry in a foreign city. *Oi gevalt!* On recovering her composure, and shaking off the shock effect of the terrible news, she paid a visit to the pawnbroker and pawned her wedding-ring. With Carl's help, a money-order was then sent to the address in New York City given by Sam. He came home, exactly a year after his departure. Sure, his confidence was dented and he had lost a little of his self-assurance and cockiness; but these returned soon after his home-coming.

I never got my dollar.

Carl and Sam, together, could have provided enough material for several short stories, plays and musicals, enough drama and comedy, violence and sex, to satisfy the most critical of critics, and the most fastidious of theatre-goers. You know something? That Shakespeare fellow was right when he said:

> All the world's a stage
> And all the men and women merely players.

I have known for many years, through long observation, that truth IS stranger than fiction.

I shall let you look into the Caplan kaleidoscope. Herein you will see a series or medley of events, pictures and scenes (not what the butler saw which was rather mundane) which are only a part of my memory store. The flashing light shows a bedroom – our bedroom – with its two beds. On one, Jerry, Sam and I, on the other Carl and Louis. We are all propped-up in a sitting position, with pillows at back. The solitary electric-bulb is burning, for we have recently emerged from the 'gas-mantle' age. Carl is putting a dart into a Diana airgun; he takes careful aim – then Bingo! He has shot a large moth and pinned its body to the ceiling. Three others likewise executed, one in flight. Being summer, the window is wide open. The room is humid, sticky, almost like an evening in Singapore. This apart, five young men in one room require a lot of ventilation. Carl is really a fine marksman – an excellent shot. Yet he is the only one who wears glasses. At each successful shot, he makes a remark, as an expression of his 'modesty', such as:

'You must understand, gentlemen, this calls for a good eye, a steady hand – and of course, a total disregard for mother's nicely-painted ceiling. Our venerable brother Sam . . .'(he never misses a dig) 'would be unable to perform such an act of skill, owing to his debauchery.'

Sam mutters – 'You're a four-eyed, big-headed ox.'

An argument then develops, with Louis, always the mediator, desperately trying to bring about calm and reason. Jerry and I are too frightened and too young to take part. Sam jumps into their bed in an attempt to intimidate Carl. The iron-sprung bed cannot take the sudden impact and extra weight. It collapses to the floor, with the three struggling youths and a flurry of arms and legs. Pandemonium reigns. The noise has brought my parents and sisters into our room. With cries of '*oi gevalt*' and '*keender! keender!*' from Mum and Dad and screams of fear from the girls, the three bodies eventually manage to extricate themselves from the floor. Sam's naked body emerges last, for he has fallen underneath the combined weight of the other two. On seeing him in the nude, the girls' screams of fear turn into roars of laughter. A fitting anti-climax.

The scene has changed. Carl sits at a table, engrossed in his work. He is working on the making of a crystal-wireless set; he is one of the first men in Scotland to produce one at home. On his head sits a metal band with ear-phones attached. His long, thin musician-fingers deftly manipulate wires and crystal. Suddenly he emits a loud cry: 'Ma! Kids! come quickly!'

Jerry and I are first on the scene. With tremendous excitement, and shaking with the joy of achievement, of triumph, he hurriedly places one earphone apiece against our ears. 'Quiet, kids. Just listen.' And wonder of wonders, we hear dance-music, loud and clear. This was known as – 'Here's to the next time' and was followed by a man's voice which says – 'Good evening ladies and gentlemen. This is Henry Hall and orchestra...'

I may venture to add Jerry and I were probably the first Scottish kids to hear this coming over the air. What excitement! Mum and Dad kissed our 'inventor' – gave him several *mazeltovs*. The atmosphere was vibrant. A new era had begun.

The kaleidoscope is still whirling on. Louis has sent me to deliver a message to his friend whose family occupy a flat on the first floor, below us. The door is opened by his mother. She was at this time a large, middle-aged woman whose name I shall not mention. She is in usual house attire... white blouse open at front, with large breasts ready to jump into view, no frock or dress, but long blue bloomers elasticated at waist and at knee ends. I was in awe of her, as were indeed most the kids around. I am invited into the house, the kitchen, and told to 'Vait!' Her son is in the lavatory. On the kitchen-table stands a large piss-pot, next to half a loaf of bread and the remains of a meal. I am then invited to sit down, 'have a cup of tea and a nice biscuit'. Naturally, I decline. As they say in Yorkshire – 'There's nowt as queer as folk.'

The picture changes once more. Sam was the first member of our family to buy a car. He was then the most affluent. The vehicle was bought, second-hand, at a car-auction in the Gallowgate. It wasn't cheap. It cost £2.10... (this being equal to a tradesman's pay for a 49-hour week).

With much pride he washed the car prior to taking all the family for a run into the country. Crowds of kids and adults watched in admiration. This was a novelty, something to talk about – the Caplans have a car. The only other car-owner in the whole street was Doctor Gladstone Robertson.

All went well until we were within sight of Balloch (Loch Lomondside), some 18 miles from Glasgow. The rear near-side wheel's brake-lining was on fire. We all jumped out in alarm. Sparks and flames were threatening to spread to the tyre. There was no other car in sight. And of course we did not possess a fire-extinguisher. Carl took command. He advised the ladies to walk towards the town and wait for the men at the first hotel. To the boys, and Dad, he issued an order. 'All of us will PEE on the burning wheel.' Which we did. And the fire went out. Crude, yes. Efficient . . . absolutely.

Another set of pictures appear;

Carl had got home after a long day. He had been in the factory, from 8 in the morning till 6 p.m. He had rushed home, had a hasty meal, changed into evening-dress, and gone to the Capital cinema at Ibrox - to play in the orchestra until the last show, ending at 10.30 p.m. He was now very tired. At this time of night he always enjoyed fish and chips, as opposed to a good, traditional Jewish meal, whether that be chicken soup with *kneidlech* (a type of doughball) fish latkes or potato latkes (a *latki* being a fritter) *lokshen* (noodles) or sandwiches made with baigels (rolls) and salmon.
   Etty would normally volunteer to go to the fish and chip shop in Norfolk Street. At this time there was a kosher chip shop in the district, but being further than Mitchell's - and it being rather late at night - Mum was loath to ask her to go too far. Many drunks would be about. They could be troublesome. It so happened Mitchell's was very clean, and their quality of a high standard. I realise what I am about to say is funny, but it gives an insight to Carl's eccentricity. Before she arrived back at the house, my sister would do as most kids would. She opened the bag carefully and pinched a chip or two. While she handed the goods to mother, who opened the cover and grease paper within to place on a plate, Carl had detected a chippy smell from her breath. He raged, and condemned her as a thief. He made a drama of it, much to the poor girl's consternation and humiliation. What a bloody carry-on, by a man who was educated and who would claim to be a 'man of the world'. His behaviour, in relation to Etty, was boorish, bullying, and uncalled for. He was a classical example of a brilliant man, an academic, who lacked commonsense and elementary manners.
   She continued to go at night for his fish and chips, and on return had to submit to the smelling of her breath. I have often thought: if his conduct be the result of a good education, then I am glad to be just an ordinary guy.

On occasion Mum would have to visit her sister Sophie, or one of her sisters-in-law. She would usually leave the house after we had come home

from school at four p.m. Our tea would be prepared and ready to eat.
Sam was put in charge of us, for Dad and Carl were at work. She would
ask Sam to look after his brothers and sisters, and have the house clean
and tidy on her return. Sam was bribed. A shiny sixpence was his fee.
That money was never shared. After tea was eaten (or drunk) he issued
orders. None of us would dare disobey. 'All hands to the job.' Pails, hot-
water, soap, dusters, brushes; a task for all of us – except himself. He
was the 'gaffer', the foreman, the boss. He was not averse to giving slaps
and pushes when he considered them necessary.

Etty was the main 'fall-guy', being a big girl and next to Sam in age. To
her fell the heaviest chores . . . scrubbing of floors, carrying full pails of
water, and so on. Meanwhile our lord and master would sit and drink
one cup of tea after another, barking orders from time to time. If we
completed the job in time, and to his satisfaction, then and only then,
would he allow us to wash our hands and go out to play. By the way,
Jerry and I got it easy; we just moved a chair or two if required. On
Mum's return, at about 6 p.m., Sam would be beaming, showing her 'all
the work he had done' – and putting his hand out for 'a few more
pennies, Ma.'

I must not give the impression of being without sin. For I too had been
tainted, and not without blemish. I make no excuse by saying I was a
mere apprentice to Sam. He led, and I followed like a little sheep. In fact,
Mum had reprimanded me many times for being Sam's lap-dog, saying
that I was too much under my brother's rotten influence. I was ever silent
on that score, for it was the truth. For me, my attachment was a
love/hate affair. I loved and hated him. I loved him for his special
attention towards me; he made me feel important – if only to him. He
supplied me with money – fourpence a week to be precise. That sum
augmented the meagre penny per week given by Dad.

As in all things, a price has to be paid for favours given. And I paid,
with interest. I had to be at his beck and call, night and day. He often got
me out of bed, late on an evening, to run an errand. Perhaps I was sent to
the chippie, or café up the street to fetch cigarettes, or lemonade, or to go
at full haste and deliver a note to one of his girl-friends; or maybe he
simply wanted to chastise me for something I had done, as for instance
when I inadvertently got him into hot water by mentioning to Mum that I
had seen him with a girl (an infamous young woman) after he had
faithfully promised not to see her again, ever.

It was handy on a few occasions, having his muscle to back me up,

Like the time when the school bully threw the dreaded challenge at me: 'See me up the lane at 4 o'clock. I'm gonna smash your Jew-face.' That lane at the back of our school was the venue for all fights. To disregard such a challenge was unthinkable. I would be 'sent to Coventry'; and be considered as a coward for the rest of my school-days. Furthermore, the whole of the school would be there, anticipating spattering of blood and screams of agony.

Besides, I too had a reputation to keep. Jerry looked up to me as *his* hero; the rapport and affinity between him and me transcended all things; with us it was true brotherly love, which exists to this day, with no ulterior motives... no payments... no conditions. Mutual respect was the basis of our strength. We shared the same interests. We played together. We even came home from school together... both with dirty pants. This had happened far too often. In many respects, we behaved and acted like twins.

Came the big fight. For me, one of many. I had no idea why Hughie McNab wanted to change my face, for I liked it the way it was. I suppose a bully doesn't need an excuse. I put it down to the necessity for him to exhibit his physical superiority from time to time, in order to maintain his 'throne' and his following of stooges. He figured on me being 'easy meat'.

That fight made school history. It lasted longer than any previous battle. Jerry informed me later, tearfully, that it had taken almost twenty minutes. I was surprised, for I had lost all count of time and had felt it had gone on for a week. I was covered in blood; my clothes were torn; I was completely exhausted. I had lost two teeth, one eye was closed, and an ear torn. Yet, McNab fared far worse. When he got home, his mother rushed him to the Royal Infirmary, wherein he was kept for two days. He suffered severe bruising, lacerations, and a dislocated elbow, plus shock and the loss of blood. You may ask, how can young boys be so vicious? I do not know. I was never proud of myself after a fight. All I can say, in mitigation, was that to my knowledge I was never the one to start trouble. For I was a small boy. Today I am only a wee man, 5 feet 4 inches in height. My temperament does not allow me to refuse a challenge, especially if my race is insulted. Today, I would give my life for the state of Israel.

Anyway, where does Sam come into this? Well, two days later Mr McNab and his elder son called at my home. Only Mum was at home. They wanted me – or should I say, my blood. Mum was devastated, almost hysterical. She tried to reason with them, to point out that I too was injured. More important, young McNab had thrown out the challenge to me . . . he was a hooligan, a no-gooder, a *baitz* . . . . This only served to make them more angry. They said they would be back in an hour. What could poor Mum do? We had no phone in those days, otherwise she would have rung the police. She could not leave the house as she was in the middle of making our evening meal.

In desperation she ran down the stairs and called at a neighbour (whose young son happily was at home). She briefly told them what had occurred, and asked the lad to look for me and tell me that I must go to the police station and not come home without an officer for protection.

The boy found me at the sweet shop across the street, and told me of the drama. I thanked him and told him to tell my mother not to worry, I knew what to do. I did. I ran to Coburg Street, saw Sam at the corner with some of his mates, and blurted out what had happened. With Sam and four friends I marched towards our street. And would you believe it? we came face to face with the McNabs. I recognised them, for Hughie had the same ugly face as his father and brother.

Sam: 'Good evening, cunts! So you've come round here to bash-up my young brother? Now I can see why your little bastard is such a rat. He takes after his poxy old man – and pig-faced brother. But you won't be disappointed. You come looking for a fight – and you're going to get one. Let's all go into a back-yard.'

Mr Mac's face was worth seeing. He began to stammer something about a mistake being made . . . that he had merely come to ask me to leave his boy alone . . . leave *his* boy alone . . . what a bloody liar.

Sam was not taken in, of course. But he was angry. Very angry. 'I'm going to do to you what my kid brother did to the rat.'

He realised the two men would not fight. They were obviously terrified (can you blame them?) Without more ado his fists went into action. The older McNab fell to the ground with a broken jaw. The son tried to run away, but was held roughly by the boys. He began to plead for mercy.

'You can't blame me, mister, honest. I had to come along with my old man. Ah've got nothing tae dae wi' it. Ah swear that, so ah do.'

Sam stared hard at the fellow, who was about his own age. 'Well, I believe you, for some reason. I'm going to let you go. But, if you ever cause any more trouble, in any way to my family, or if I ever see you near our house, then I swear I'll kill you both. Now fuck-off and take this old shitbag with you.'

With that he kicked the moaning man on the thigh, then leaned towards him – and spat on his face.

Now, by way of change, let us move from drama to humour. Remember, that 'scope is still recording scenes from the past.

Let me tell you about Duncan Murchie. He lived in our close. His sister Dolly and our Etty are the best of friends. I still get randy when I think of that voluptuous female, as she was then. Duncan was my age, a cheery, ever-smiling boy. He attended a different school, had his own friends, and for some reason he seldom played with my crowd. On Friday afternoons, *erev* Sabbath (before the Sabbath) Jewish mothers were always busy preparing and cooking meals for the week-end. By Law, orthodox Jews must not light fires or cookers over Sabbath, which lasts from dusk on Friday, till sunset on Saturday. Though we did not observe custom, generally, as we were not orthodox, mother did her best to conform in many ways. Certainly, in common with our Jewish neighbours, she cooked chicken, with all the trimmings – fried fish-cakes and/or latkes (potato-fritters).

Coming home from school on a Friday afternoon, the delicious smell emanating from our kitchen permeated the entire tenement. One Friday, as I was passing Murchie's door, Duncan appeared.

'Have you any comics to change with me, Jack?'

'Sure I have . . . I've got some *Rovers*, *Funny Wonders*, and maybe an old *Wizard* or two. Come up with me and I'll sort them out.'

So we climbed the stairs. His nose began to rotate like a rabbit's.

'Gee! That wonderful smell again. Is your mother cooking?'

We entered the house. Indeed that smell did stimulate the gastric juices. Mum was frying the fish-cakes. Our eyes were glued to the large plate into which she was placing the cooked ones. Turning round to greet us, she saw the look of expectation in our faces.

'All right boys. You can have one each.'

From that moment onwards, Master Murchie was hooked. He raved about that delicacy each and every time we met. He gave me no peace. 'How is it made? What is it made of? How often does your mum make these dishes?' And so on. This introduction to *Yiddishy essen* (food) happened to coincide with Sam's sojourn in America. Consequently, I was poorer by fourpence each week. So I had a quiet talk with young Murchie, and we came to a business arrangement. He would pay me a penny for a potato latki, twopence for a fish-cake.

A month later my mother took me to task:

'It's a funny thing, my son, but I've noticed that, when you're about on a Friday, my counting is all wrong. Either I'm going blind, or there's a ghost in the house who eats my latkis and fish-cakes. Maybe, from now on, it will go away. Would you say so?'

A clever, shrewd lady. The 'ghost' was now exorcised, without fuss or argument, and I had lost a good source of revenue.

By this time the reader will have noticed, and perhaps wondered . . . the writer is a member of a large family, yet so far only four characters have been on parade: Mum, Dad, Sam and Carl. To my mind this is based on the proportion, or degree of influence in relation to my formative years. The all-important impressionable years.

Sam takes precedence over both Carl and Dad, actually, in terms of influence. Carl was destined to take over the duties and responsibilities of his father from an early age. He toiled long hours, and devoted himself to Mother's needs. To say he was both administrative and executive officer to the family – and legal adviser – would be nearer the mark. Consequently, he had no time for the younger members of the family.

All through the bad years, the hungry twenties and thirties, it was he who substantially augmented father's small wages. It is true to say Dad did make a lot of money when, for a year or two during World War I, he had his own little factory and a War Department contract for uniforms. Regrettably, he could not cope. He was illiterate and possessed a limited knowledge of English, and had a partner who was unscrupulous; he was utterly vulnerable, a lamb to the slaughter, taken in by a rotter.

Again, my Dad liked a drink. He also had too many 'friends' who were cadgers, moochers, sharks. Old Morris the Jew was an easy 'touch'. Alas! He was. It would have been entirely different had Carl and Sam been grown men. But then they were just two little boys.

To brother Carl, again, goes the grateful, heartfelt thanks from us three 'kids' . . . me, Jerry and Anna. Without him so many Christmases would have been just another day. Mum would have managed a bar of chocolate and some fruit to each of us, but Carl, and Carl alone, deputised for Santa Claus. Every Christmas we could expect at least one toy apiece. A cap-pistol one year, a peashooter another, and on one memorable festive-day (as a result of an extra gig or two, or a new violin-pupil), our Santa splashed out. There was a big Hornby train set, working by battery, with a set of rails to match, for Jerry. And for me, there was a brand new Diana air-rifle with a packet of darts. The trouble was, our big brothers played more with those toys than we did, after a while.

Sam, on occasion, played his part by taking us to the annual Kelvin Hall Circus and Carnival – a wonderful treat. We got sweets, ice-cream and chocolates too.

At this juncture I have an experience to relate, perhaps one which ought to be recorded in the Guinness Book of Records.

At the Carnival, 1925, when I was 10, Sam had first bought us large ice-creams and had decided, before going into the circus, to take the three of us to the menageries (at an extra cost of two pence, if I remember right). Well, all went well. Jerry and Anna stood watching the swaying elephants in complete fascination, and Sam took me by the hand across to the cage of a huge lion. In typical, restless fashion the animal kept going round and round, back and forth, up and down. Suddenly, it stopped and lifted its leg against the boarded end of the cage. My ice-cream and my face was spattered by the animal's urine – which had ricochetted from the wall on to me. But at the time I had not realised what it was. I gazed upwards, to the ceiling of the hall, and complained, almost tearfully: 'Sammy, the rain came down. My face is wet – and so is my ice-cream.' Sam howled with laughter, as did those people who were around the cage at the same time. It is not everyone who can boast of being pissed on by a lion.

As you may have gathered, Carl and Sam were two totally different persons. Carl was the studious one, the worrier, the hard-worker, who had a very special attachment to Mother, and who forever gave one the impression that he was near to a nervous breakdown. On the other hand there was Sam, not friendly-disposed towards any form of work, yet seldom without money. He was mean of temper, ever ready for fisti-cuffs with all and sundry; was fond of gambling on horses, dogs and cards; would spend a lot of money drinking with his mates; but would begrudge paying his small contribution to the upkeep of our home. He always demanded the best food available and the use of our big room every Sunday night for gambling with his cronies. No one would dare disapprove. His Sunday night 'casino' was a typical ploy for making easy gelt. Not only was he a very good all-round ace with playing-cards, specifically at the popular games of the evening, pontoon, brag, and poker, but an added sideline of his was the large money-box placed on the centre of the table. At the end of every game – or every round of a game – the winner had to insert threepence into the 'kitty'. Sam explained to the players that the proceeds would be paid to mother for the use of the room. Little did they know that it was for the pocket of Mr S. Caplan. I had witnessed Sam emptying that box many times, and it always contained several pounds, a fortune in those days.

Whereas Carl demonstrated his affection for Mum, Sam was more partial to Dad. They worked together for many years; they would drink together on an evening. Sam would place bets on the horses for him, as Dad was unable to write a slip, nor comprehend form. If an easy pound was to be made, then Sam was in on it. Yes, he spent money on girls, took them to good restaurants, would buy them silk-stockings too. But give his sisters anything, never! Apart from my fourpence a week, his brothers likewise never ever saw a penny from him. For all those things, I despised him, and was too afraid of him to raise a voice in protest. Until the 'big fight'. I shall come to that shortly. I would, firstly, introduce Louis, my senior by three years.

Louis

Brother Louis should follow sister Ethel, in these pages for she is older than he. It is with no disrespect to her that I give him preference. I am just giving priority to those who were most instrumental in shaping my life and my general outlook in all matters appertaining to living.

Louis had more in common with Carl than with Sam, Jerry or me. In fact, he was in many respects an enigma. He was at all times placid, unruffled, cool, calm and collected. Dare I say it? I considered him to be the most unemotional person I have ever known. When tempers were aroused at home, and dirty names were bandied back and forth, Louis's was the quiet voice of reason which held sway, melting the fires of passion. And yet, underneath that veneer of stoicism there lay a devious imp. It is said that 'still waters run deep'. I for one could never penetrate his thoughts, could never really feel comfortable with him. Not one of the family really knew, for sure, what his innermost feelings were.

Completely out of character at times, he was known to throw a verbal dart, in the shape of a pungent remark, and shatter one's ego. It happened with me, when at the age of 18, I took up pen and paper to make a reply to the readers' letters column of the *Glasgow Evening Times*, in answer to a man who supported the rise of Nazism in Germany. That 'gentleman' admitted to being a member of Moseley's British Union of Fascists. At the time, I was a member of the Young Communist League (until I recovered my sanity). My letter was published in full, and I was pleased with myself, for two good reasons: my first literary effort had been accepted; and I had had a good swipe at the evils of fascism, judging by the stream of supporting letters which followed. On asking Louis if he had seen my letter he withdrew his pipe from his mouth, his eyes narrowed, and he replied:

'Yes I did! And here's my advice to you: you must write from your brain, not your heart. In my opinion, you have ambition – but no ability.'

Fair enough! Every man is entitled to his opinion. But why should mine be invalid?

I retorted angrily: 'If I have ambition sans ability then we make a good team. For you have ability, for sure – and *no* ambition.'

On reflection, both Louis and Carl had one thing in common, this being a knack for giving others an inferiority complex.

Possibly, Louis had in mind the old proverb: 'It is better to think what we say than to say what we think.'

In the same year, 1933, Louis opened a small printing-shop in the Gallowgate. He was not a printer himself, but had been with the advertising department of the *Jewish Echo* for a while. He had also taken piano lessons for three years, when a pupil of Hutcheson Grammar School for Boys, and had abruptly terminated his musical venture, though it had cost Mum a small fortune. If my memory serves me correctly, he had also worked for a while in the office of a chartered accountant, but to no avail.

The actual printing was produced by a retired man who had been a compositor all his life. He (a Mr Carswell) was happy to return to work. He was of the old school, complete with stiff collar and bowler hat, and he was a good all-rounder. It so happened that the firm I had been working for (manufacturers of rubber-coats, ground-sheets, etc.) had closed down the Glasgow Office and factory, and I was without work. My mother had a talk with Louis. She was worried about my future. It was decided that he would take me in as an apprentice to old Bill (Mr Carswell). (I should point out that had it not been for my sister Etty, who had financed this latest venture, there would have been no printing business.) Simultaneously to starting a business, Louis started courting – and it can also be said he was piling-up a lot of trouble for himself. So much, too much, was happening to him all at once.

Unlike Sam, or even me for that matter, he could admire a girl from afar, and leave it at that. Jerry was the same, their blood was lukewarm. With Sam and me, it was ever simmering. I cannot remember our Louis having had an amorous affair, except for an occasional romp in the hay with an attractive little tram-conductress called Cathie. She was his 'standby' ride.

He did, however, fall heavily for the young woman who is now his wife. For her, he dropped everything – including his pants. Mum said of him: 'He's gone *meshugge* (daft)...the *shiksa* comes from nowhere, we know nothing about her, or her family, and she looks like a *shmatte* (rag).'

Mum's anger and frustration was based, not entirely on the fact of the girl being a Gentile, but on the great expectations she had anticipated for the boy. Though unsettled as yet, work-wise, she felt he, of all others, would follow Carl's footsteps and carve a niche for himself, a good career in one of the professions. In truth, all Jewish mothers want their sons to be doctors, solicitors, scientists and musicians. Poverty and hardship are merely obstacles to be overcome. It has to be admitted that 'Success more sweet when challenge is beat.' The general concensus of opinion at the time was that Louis had lost all reason. As Sam aptly put it, in his inimitable way – 'He is completely cunt-struck!' I knew of no one who liked the girl.

Today, they are living quite happily in Australia. I would be treading a tightrope – or at the least could be accused of insensitivity – were I to speak more of this particular sister-in-law.

To get back to business, so to speak. I worked hard. I was glad of being given an opportunity to learn a good trade. With diligence and determination (and attending Stow Street College of Printing) I was considered as an asset and a useful member of the firm. The name given to it was 'Publicity Printing Co.' I can't remember for certain but I think my wage was £2 per week.

Louis had now taken in his first partner, Hyman Silverman. He was a nice, cheery fellow, though not entirely too fond of work. But we got on together. The firm was growing, now there were Louis, Hymie, old man Carswell, and I. Then we took on, as apprentice number two, a very nice lad named Willie Black. Young Black and I became good friends. Both of us concentrated more on the machines, as opposed to the compositing (type-setting). Our plant consisted of two platens – which included a Heidelberg, and a Double-Crown Miehle, capable of poster work. We had lots of type-cases, and miscellaneous equipment. Sadly, however, it was a very small shop, though we had utilised the cellar as a paper-store.

Louis was an excellent 'traveller'. He had made many contacts, many friends, and as he quickly learned the technicalities such as paper-sizes, weights, and the varying processes involved, the business was rapidly developing.

There were times, in the beginning, when very little work came in. It was depressing. Hymie and Louis would borrow two shillings from Old Bill, and then would say – 'We're off to see a customer in Hamilton (12 miles away) so we will not be back before 5 o'clock.' I later learned that, when they went off together in that fashion, it was to go to the pictures. The Argyle Cinema was then just down the road. Can you blame them?

Old Bill was then in charge. For him it was like the old days, being a 'gaffer' in a 'jobbing-shop' letterpress. My duties included answering the telephone. I can look back with pride on recalling how well I had adapted myself to this trade, and all aspects involved. Much credit goes to old Bill. At times he would pull me and Willie across the room by the ears, in way of reprimand for some demeanour – but he sure had printing-ink in his veins. (An expression used to define a person who was a natural . . . a top-notcher.)

An order comes through per telephone. I answer. A customer requires, as soon as possible, let us say – 1,000 handbills (leaflets) Size . . . 8 × 5 . . . octavo. Printed one side, black ink only. How much? I glance at the price-list near by and quote cost.

I would usually follow instinct, and knew when it was safe to add on an extra shilling. Old Bill and I would then work out how much paper would be required, in quires. We had many reams of newsprint in stock — so there would be no need for me, in that case, to call round to one of our local suppliers. After arriving at the quantity of paper needed (allowing for wastage) I would descend to the cellar, bring up the paper, and cut it to size on our huge hand-powered guillotine whilst the two others would be hand-setting the copy handed them by me on a clip, for their guidance. Usually I too would grab a setting-stick and Bill would instruct me as to the fount best suited to the job. When the setting was finished, the whole typematter was then locked securely into a metal frame, called a 'chase'. From then on, the ball was in my court once more. This was to prepare the machine for action. Ink . . . black. Rollers in position. Make ready on cylinder appropriate. Pull first proof. Read over and check carefully for errors, either grammatical or type-wise. On being satisfied that all was well and in order – switch on machine (clear the decks, as it were) and run-off the job.

As those bills were for speedy delivery, it was necessary to put a quick drying chemical into the ink, usually by means of a spray. I would then pack them into a neat, brown-paper parcel, stick on one of our PPC labels, with customer's name and address clearly visible, write out an invoice – then presto! I'd grab my jacket, and parcel, then nip round to the customer with it – by foot (shank's pony). Talk about 'speedy Gonzales'.

All this would have been done within two hours of receiving the order. It should be explained that such efficiency is practically impossible nowadays, for many reasons, chiefly because of what is termed as 'lines of demarcation'. A compositor is employed as a compositor; a machine-minder (printer) likewise has to keep to his own job; the print union is a strong one – and very jealously guard the many gains won by them for their members. Again, in modern times office-staff attend to all calls and enquiries; who would, or could, breach these defences?

But things were so different in my time, especially those years between the Wars. I was not just a printer's 'devil' (name applied to an apprentice) but a much exploited (though dedicated) slave.

I was fired some years after the War after an altercation with Hymie. I admit to being guilty of slapping his face, in anger. Nevertheless, I was given no monies, no form of compensation for the years of labour, of struggle, no consideration for being a pioneer of the business – which today is one of Glasgow's best-known firms in the field of print and stationery. Even the fact of being a brother of the managing director did not count. And I was at that time a married man with two children.

As my story is not concerned with the post-war years, there is no more to say on that score. But readers can appreciate my reason for feeling that brother Louis had let me down badly. He would say – 'there is no sentiment in business'. This may be so. Is the seeking of more and greater wealth (greed) a reason for tramping on compassion and humanity? I leave this with the reader to ponder.

Sister Ethel (Etty)

As the tramcars rattled, roared and clanged their way along Norfolk Street, 60 yards or so from our tenement building, and horse-driven carts rumbled by, the kids of the street were playing, shouting, yelling – or wiping snotters away with the sweat. It was after school, 4.30 on a nice afternoon.

Oh what care-free days! The innocence of children, playing, with not a care in the world. And I was one of them. It was a common sight then to see several boys, myself included, stand at the pavement's edge, take out our little 'Willies' – raise them on high for elevation, and suddenly direct the streams of urine on to the watching, gaping girls. Sure, they screamed and ran away (hoping to be chased, no doubt) then turned to us, shouting abuse; one wee lassie whom I fancied strongly (her dad was a special constable, this being the year of the General Strike, 1926) had evidently gone to some trouble by composing the following ditty:

> 'Dirty Jackie Caplan, one–two–three,
> Took out his willie, and showed it to me.
> If he won't kiss me, my heart will fail ...
> But I'll tell my daddy – and he'll go to jail.'

I reckoned this worthy of a reply:

> 'Miriam Cohen, you're a little honey –
> When next I chase you down the dunny,
> I'll fix you hard against the wall –
> Then *never* to your dad you'll call!'

The 'dunny' was the basement of a tenement. What stories to relate, if these walls could only talk.

Etty was a small girl, round-faced and fresh-complexioned. She appealed to boys who had no preference for skinny-bits. Perhaps she was never glamorous, nor did she care for make-up, but she was deliciously plump and comely. Naturally, brothers are not the best judges of a sister's sex-appeal. Her greatest attributes were a sweetness of nature, a kind disposition, being a good sister and a wonderful daughter. She was cursed (I can't think of a stronger word) with a permanent affliction, or dosage, of a complex which made her feel and left her with, a strange aura of inadequacy.

This was sad but true, and was a burden which never left her.

In every respect, she displayed a love and devotion for Mother which went far beyond the line of filial duty. Even when married, she had her husband 'pull strings' with a house-factor in order that she, Johnny and their baby girl could be housed in a flat next to Mother's.

That extra-strong attachment for Mum remained until the end of our mother's life, at the age of eighty-two. For Etty, the loss was very hard to bear. The girl's afore-mentioned burden – a phenomenon – had been perpetually exacerbated by Carl's boorish, bullying behaviour towards her.

There was seldom a dull moment in our house. At least it can be said we were lively, we were an animated lot. Perhaps we were too spirited, too energetic.

On the one hand, Carl despised Sam for his uncouthness and vulgarity; yet Carl on the other hand was profoundly intolerant of poor Etty. If she were to hum quietly a popular song of the day, or laugh gaily at something which tickled her sense of humour, then he let loose a stream of abuse and insults, shouting hysterically.

Here was a man, held in high esteem by outsiders, yet his behaviour inside the home was abominable. He and Sam were the major cause of friction. The person who suffered most as the result of the tension was poor Ma. Louis, who was the one most able, physically, to intervene and demand that commonsense prevail, merely took the line of least resistance by remaining *shtum* (quiet).

It could be said, in all truth, that both Louis and Etty lacked sparkle. Their lives were, and are, humdrum. Their personalities were mediocre, whilst Carl and Sam's were the antithesis – to the extreme.

With any of these two about, anything could happen, and usually did.

With both in close proximity, volcanic eruptions were assured. Now and again there were diversions, when one or another of the remaining five would hold the stage and would have a few moments of limelight, or glory. One example was when Etty was being bathed at home on a Sunday, at the age of 14.

Much to her embarrassment, Carl's life-long chum, Solly Bloomberg, was present in the kitchen. He was a big, happy-go-lucky jovial chap, ever smiling and pleasant. They were discussing the latest political crisis, and so paid no attention to the blushes of the cringing lass, as Mum spread soap on her. The door-bell rang. The arm-chair socialists were too engrossed in scoring advantage points over each other and so paid no attention to the bell-ringer. Mother looked at them, shook her head and sighed, then advising Etty to rinse herself with the warm water, she turned, stood up, and moved towards the door, unaware that her apron-strings were entangled with a handle of the zinc-tub . . . Etty and tub landed on the floor. In alarm she struggled to hide her body from the eyes of the young men, and in so doing knocked the vessel on to its side, leaving her *and* the soapy water on the floor.

Etty, mother's constant companion, would accompany her to the shops, to the park or cinema, and do any extra chores required at home. She worked as a tailoress with the Tailoring Guild for many years and had made lots of good friends amongst her work-mates. She would visit them at home at times, and have them spend an evening with her, with or without boy-friends. She never went dancing, or ice-skating, as did her pals. Her obsession prevented this. Quite a few young men paid her attention and wanted to court her, but rather than be out 'winching' (courting) she preferred the company of mother and the family. But that was until she met her Johnny (and that *was* his christian name). Even then, apart from the two nights a week, when they would visit a cinema or call on friends, she was ever with Mother.

John and Etty married just before the war. She would have liked to have wed a Jewish boy, primarily for mother's sake, but fate had decreed otherwise. True, eligible boys of that faith were at premium. Millions of men had been butchered during the first World War, and in post-war years, the ratio of births, as I understand it, was four to one in favour of baby girls.

None the less, she was quite contented and happy with Johnny.

Back to the street, our playing-field. Games were often interrupted by buskers, who were in the main ex-servicemen. Some were limbless but bemedalled. Even as a wee boy I had considered it an unfair exchange. A limb for a medal. A life for a telegram from the War Department stating regret.

Sometimes the juvenile gangs from Coburg Street (the 'Coburg Erin') who were Catholics , or the 'Young Cumbies' from the Cumberland Street, Protestants, would invade South Portland Street, a mainly Jewish section, with synagogue and Jewish Institute. When this occurred we usually dived into the nearest tenement to hide. On one memorable day, with Jerry and two other 'stalwarts' to back me up with moral support, I decided that a stand had to be made. My bravado emanated from the knowledge that a certain lady was looking out of her window. I had for many months loved her from afar. It was a hopeless love and one that could not possibly be reciprocated. You see, Cissie Edelman was a 'big' girl – maybe seven years my senior, and I played with Joe, her little brother. Such matters do not, *cannot*, stop the agitations, the incomprehensible simmering of an awakening of the biological urge. One may classify my action as 'showing off'. That too was possible.

Before I had time to change my mind, we were surrounded by howling, vicious young thugs, armed with belts, sticks and stones. Some were shouting such slogans as 'Fuck the Jews!' or – 'We are the Coburg Erin!' I well remember a sudden fear in my heart, for Jerry. 'Hurry! Run for it! I don't want you here.' His reply made me love him even more, if that were possible: 'If you stay, I stay.' My servility to Sam and admiration for his strength had never stopped Jerry and me being the closest of the family. On seeing me standing in defiance, arms folded and apparently so cool-looking, a hush descended. Had they only known . . . I was terrified. I needed to pee. And my pounding heart served to give me a feeling of impending doom. Jerry reckoned later that there were almost fifty of them.

What I found to be more than a little disconcerting was the feeling of drowning. My injuries had not yet completely healed from the last fight, at school, with bully McNab – only three weeks previously. Was I tempting the Gods of war? That strange feeling gnawing at my heart, causing the booming sounds . . . was this an omen of disaster?

I heard a piping voice say – 'He's the Jew leader, Tiger. Will wi' gie 'im a doin'? (thrashing) Someone else shouted: 'Smash in his bloody heid!' Nice boys, indeed. Jolly little play-mates.

And then I was face to face with the biggest, and ugliest lad ever. He made Hugh McNab, by comparison, an angelic figure. Not being Hallowe'en, it had to be his own face. I was to learn his name later,

Sammy Higgins, better known as 'Tiger' – understandably so. One look at him and the blood curdled. I learned later that his face belied his true gentleness. He was chosen as gang-chief on account of his looks and size. At heart, he was really a nice boy. I did not know this at the time.

He spoke first. 'Are yi' no feart? We can eat you an' your three pals easy. Away yees go – or yil get the message.' (a beating) Though my whole inside felt as if clutched in an icy grip, I had gone too far to retreat. Whilst relieved by the offer of the olive-branch, none the less I had to consider the implications. Reverting to the vernacular, I said:

'We'll be gled tae go, Mac, 'cos we ken it's daft tae fight. But will yi promise tae lea' us alane...no tae come looking fur trouble, eh?' Talking about cheek! Me daring to negotiate conditions, under those circumstances. Outnumbered by ten to one and scared as hell.

'Ah canny dae that? Hiv a go at me – and we'll git it o'er.'

No sooner had he said this, than I pounced. My reflex actions had never failed me, as if these were computerised signals informing me that immediate action was vital. There had been no hesitation on my part. The tactics adopted by me against the large boy was to be used in all future fights with taller opponents, with the same success. This served me well when I joined the army in 1940. No words, no threats, no waste of energy, just a grim determination to do or die. I grabbed Tiger around the waist, my chin against his chest. The element of surprise is always advantageous. He seemed bewildered by this completely unexpected turn of events. I kept tightening my grip, harder, harder. At the same time I placed a leg between his; the object being to prevent him bringing up his knee against my balls.The plan was to throw both of us to the ground – at the right moment. And I must be on top to let him take the full force of the impact. It worked to perfection. He was by then utterly winded, and hoping for a respite. This I daren't give him. As he lay, with my arms wrapped around his body, I brought down my head hard on his face, and drew a lot of blood from him. One thing was sure. He would be no prettier after this encounter. Then he shouted 'Kees! Kees!' (This is a word used by Scottish kids when they wanted a game, or activity halted. I have never been able to find out its origin.) And so ended my first meeting with young Higgins. My second meeting with him was when, on commencing my first job at a rubber factory 3 years later, he was the senior apprentice sent by the foreman to show me what my work entailed. We became good friends. He bore no malice whatsoever. Actually, I found him a pleasant companion.

After the excitement died down, and I was being congratulated by my wee brother and the others, I looked up at the Edelmans' window. My 'dream-girl' was still there, but had now been joined by members of her family. Our eyes met. She blew me a kiss. My day was made. I floated high on clouds, not of golden daffodils but of fantasies. She loves me, she had prayed for me. *I will marry her.*

My day-dream was roughly shattered. Etty with her friend Dolly Murchie, had come on the scene. They had seen over two-score Coburg Street boys, with sticks and stones, pass them quietly. No shouting. No slogans. She did not know this was a defeated 'army'. I was filthy, once again. The blood on my face was not mine – though she was not to know this. She stormed at me:

'You're just a *baitz*! A common hooligan! I don't know what we're going to do with you. Just you wait till Ma sees you – you'll catch it. In fact, I've a good mind to tell Sam on you. He'll give you what-for . . . '

Dolly handled the situation differently. 'You can't let your mother see him like this. Let's all go to my house, and we'll clean the wee man. And we'll have a wee cup of tea forbye.'

I was bundled away, each holding an arm. There was no repetition of attacks from that lot. If anything, they had become our allies. They would help us sort out other groups, if we had asked.

At this point, I should like to clarify a question or two which the reader may find puzzling, such as anti-semitism. Active or organised Jew-baiting in Glasgow was unknown. The Scots are too intelligent to fall for the propaganda then prevalent in London and other large English centres. To be sure, bitterness which did exist in some quarters between Protestants and Catholics both then and now has not affected Jews, thankfully.

Why, then did those youngsters demonstrate a hostility to Jews? Simply because some of their parents, being bigots and ignoramuses, would spout such poison at home, words of hate and defamation, wicked and unsubstantiated. The English, or for that matter, people anywhere, have not got a monopoly on stupidity and evil intent. Then as now fascists (from whatever hole they crawl) assume they have the right to spread dangerous lies to suit their own brand of politics. Yet they would deny others the right to reject their filth. I am convinced, however, that the parents concerned did have an enemy - poverty, and this was aggravated by having too many mouths to feed.

Author's Observations

Next in line comes yours truly...myself. As I have already infiltrated into the picture in so many ways, there is not too much to add. As a narrator I have much to learn. I tend to be guilty of deviating from the subject matter, this being tantamount to stealing the thunder from the individual under scrutiny. I can only plead, in mitigation, inexperience. As humans, none of us are perfect. Though people of Carl's calibre would vehemently deny this by saying: 'I am!' Clever as hell, yes; sharp as a needle, yes; knowing most answers to given problems, yes. But, no man or woman can attain the ultimate in relation to such virtue. Here again I am reminded of the words uttered by a sage: 'The wise man seeks Perfection - only the fool would expect to find it.'

I am a cynic by nature. I always look in both directions when I have to cross a one-way street. As Cromwell aptly said: 'Put your trust in God, if you so wish - but keep your powder dry.'

Talking of Cromwell - he was nobody's fool. Though he ultimately lost his head under the executioner's axe, whilst that head was on his shoulders he did use it well. For it was he who allowed Jews to re-enter Britain. He was motivated by the bankruptcy of the country, to be sure, and the poverty of the masses, not to mention the need for an injection of wise counselling (unrelated to politics), and the revival of trade and commerce.

As an ex-Gorbalite born and bred amidst them - a hotchpotch of races: Scots, Irish, Jews and Italians - I can speak with some knowledge of my colourful neighbours and fellow Jews.

You may ask 'what made the Gorbals different from other centres of large Jewish populations in the UK?' Indeed, cold facts and figures can be found in any public reference library. But such information given is clinical. It is without warmth and vitality, or if you like, it is soul-less.

It has to be said. In cities wherein only a handful of Jews lived, such as Edinburgh, Dundee or Perth, or in towns like Paisley or Kilmarnock, there was not the same atmosphere or vibrancy, excitement or interest. In all truth, no place in Scotland could be compared to the Gorbals of Glasgow. It was unique. Take Gorbals Cross on a Sunday. This was the rendezvous for every ethnic group. It was a hive of activity where men chatted in English, Yiddish and Gaelic. All Jewish shops were open, as our Sabbath is on Saturday. Here and there Polish, Russian and Italian could also be heard. Men argued, discussed, made business deals. Women did their shopping, gossiped, then went home to prepare the Sunday meals for their families. Cycling-groups passed by on their way to the country. Golfers, with bags of clubs over shoulders, boarded tramcars which would take them to many of the numerous golf-clubs in and around the city.

A Glasgow chief constable once remarked: 'Life would be nice and tranquil in this city if all our citizens behaved as well as the Jewish people.'

Around the corner, in Rutherglen Road, a small knot of people would gather outside the office of the Hebrew Burial Society, awaiting the hearse and accompanying vehicles. At the cemetery, a burial-service cannot commence without at least ten men (a *minyan* or quorum). Well, occasionally, it did happen that a shortage of male Jews was evident. To offset this, there were usually a few well-known local characters hanging about, anticipating their presence being required. It would be an outing for them. A ride in a hired limousine or private car to the cemetery and back, and a good drink, with a meal, at the home of some relative of the deceased.

Always perfect harmony reigned. Beefy Patricks and Michaels, small and dapper Sollys, Izzys and Abies. Here and there a Marco or Giuseppe.

The younger men amongst the Jews often roared with laughter when the older men, the original immigrants, talked of some experience or incident, for the young bucks were first generation British and educated. Like, for instance, when my Dad, proud of his craft, and his special friendly relations with a good customer, a Mr Watson, was saying: 'My goot friend, Mr Vatson, vas so pleased vit his suit – he brought a friend to my house for me to make him von. Vell, di friend said to me "I vant a good job vit it – just like you did for Tom Vatson." But I told di man, don't vorry, don't vorry, I vill make you di best "police force" in Glasgow.' These were the days when the wearing of *plus fours* was common.

Jewish craftsmen were, if nothing else, meticulous. They may have lacked a proper use of the King's English, and a knowledge of the finer points of etiquette and accepted behaviour in conforming to certain standards. They (or most of them) had never received a formal education, so at times they landed in trouble.

Mr Finkelstein had been given the contract to paint the interior of the convent. Half-way through the work, he was called to the office of Mother Superior. Telling him to be seated comfortably, she then spoke: 'Mr Finkelstein, to be sure, I have no complaints with your work. But I must ask you to stop washing your hands in the Holy water, and please, please, do not refer to me as Mother *Shapiro*.'

The Gorbals of old was highly populated, the streets ever-crowded. It throbbed with life. Robert Burns (that great and prolific writer) wrote:

> It's comin' yet for a' that,
> That Man to Man the world o'er
> Shall brothers be for a' that.

This fine sentiment found breeding-ground in the Gorbals.

To many English people (too many) the Gorbals is synonymous with gangs, razor-slashing and furtive shadows in the night, with ladies of easy virtue stalking lanes and back-streets. This is absolute rubbish. The unsavoury label is due, mainly, to the media . . . and to writers of fiction.

I have lived in Glasgow most of my life, in the very heart of the Gorbals. But I have never seen a gang-fight, as such, with grown men involved. Of course we did have gangs, as do as other places: London, Birmingham, Manchester, Liverpool, Cardiff, etc. (Why should the English, particularly, have a monopoly of gangs and criminals?) With apologies to Winston Churchill I venture to mis-quote: 'Never has so much rubbish been written by a few, against so many.' The good folk of the Gorbals have been maligned for too long. Certainly, when a boy, I had fights with juvenile delinquents, some of whom belonged to 'gangs'. But this is not what the media have in mind.

Adult gangs did fight, but not with innocent people or bystanders.

They fought with each other, usually in pre-arranged venues such as open spaces, or parks. Most of these fights were in the name of 'religion'... Catholics v. Protestants; Rangers supporters against Celtic fans. I should say, it was the scum fringes of each group, not the majority of decent followers of the game.

The only razors I had seen in action belonged to my Dad and older brothers, when shaving.

The Scots, Irish and Jews had so much in common. It's well-known that the Scots, in general, have no love for the English – for good reason; that the Irish, to this day, consider themselves at war with England. Let me qualify that by saying... some Irishmen. And as for the Jew, no one can deny that his whole history is one of bitterness, persecution, and tragedy.

In that small area, the Gorbals, a link was forged. Three races had united. Though belonging to different religions and coming from differing backgrounds, an affinity grew and developed. It was common for any one tenement to have Jews, Scots and Irish families living together. Verily, the Cohens and Kellys, strengthened by the Stewarts or McDonalds.

As a postscript to this, I can say in all sincerity: 'Some of my best friends are Gentiles.'

The Scots do tend to take most things seriously. Politics, sports (especially football), religion, good strong beer, and malt whisky. I must admit, that they carry a huge chip on their shoulders with regard to the English.

And yet, they are perhaps the most generous, the most warm-hearted people in the universe. Pay no attention to all the stories of mean Scots, or for that matter, mean Jews. These are myths. This brings me back to one of the many things shared by all three races. They are not averse to telling jokes against themselves. I have learned to trust people who can laugh at themselves.

The Scots are individuals in a race for self-assertion and identity. The Jews are a race *possessing* self-assurance – and wrongly identified. Do give this a little thought. As for the Irish, bless 'em, well... sure and bejabbers, they'll be back in the morning to tell us what they're having for dinner today... And to give us our invitations to the meal.

During the Spanish Civil War (1936–38) many of my friends left

Glasgow to join the British battalion of the International Brigade. At 21 years of age at the outbreak of this, I was familiar with the intrigues involved, the cowardly politics of the west in its neutral attitude – particularly Britain – and the terrible dangers to the world if the democratically-elected Spanish government were to collapse, as did happen.

The poverty-stricken Spanish people were attempting to shake off the shackles and feudalism imposed mainly by the Catholic church. General (butcher) Franco led the Falange (fascist) troops, supported by thousands of Moors and Italian infantry, fascism being the brain-child of Mussolini, Hitler's ally. German planes used this war as 'bloody good practice' or exercises in training Nazi airmen for the World War being prepared by both dictators.

On hearing of the huge losses inflicted upon the almost defenceless people, the bombing of cities such as Guernica and Toledo – cities with no military targets – and the wholesale massacres of men, women and children, I decided to join my friends there.

I was wondering how to explain matters to Mother . . . should I go without fuss, simply leaving a note behind? Or would it better to speak with Carl and Sam first – let them explain and give comfort to Ma?

Then the worst happened. Britain imposed immediate sanctions – the name used for officially discouraging men and materials from entering Spain. The government here was paying lip-service to European fascism. And the world paid for this later – in World War 2.

The radio and newspapers gave this announcement wide coverage. There were some protests. Frankly, and regretfully, most British people could not care less. It was not their fight. So what (as they in their ignorance saw it) does it matter if a few 'commies' were being shot in Spain?

I felt frustrated, angry, utterly dejected. Hitler and his henchman Mussolini were overjoyed. They were grateful to the British leaders for their 'understanding'. Entry into Spain through the Pyrenees was now blocked too.

About a week after this sanctions bombshell, the 'Friends of Spain' organisation announced that a Public Meeting was being held in the city's St. Andrew's Hall, at this time the largest venue in Glasgow. All 'friends' and sympathisers of General Franco's 'war on communism' would be most welcome. Accompanied by a friend, Tommy Clarke, I joined the large demonstration of protest organised by the Scottish

Labour Movement. I cannot be sure, but I think one of the celebrities leading this march was 'Manny' Shinwell, later to become Lord Shinwell. Many other well-known figures were to be seen.

The police were out in force, everywhere. It was known that many of them had sympathy with Moseley and his verminous bunch. This was not surprising, for a weak government cannot be expected to have an efficient police-service, or army. Mounted police were also in the thick of it, riding up and down, shouting at the marchers and attempting to discourage spectators from joining the demonstration. I saw one man being struck by a mounted officer's baton, picked up by some shocked onlookers and given first-aid; I heard a policeman say to another: 'I'd shoot the whole fuckin' lot.'

Someone had said that admission into the hall was by ticket only. I do not know if this were so, or not. I do know that Tommy and I managed to enter by a side door. We had observed a uniformed man standing there, on the inside. He was a 'blackshirt' (fascist) and was one of fifty who had come up from London to act as stewards. We watched him closely from a distance. Then, when he seemed to have left his post, we furtively approached the door, noting that the disappearance of his reflection on the glass door-top was due to the man being called over to the booking office window at the foyer. Someone there was having a heated argument with an official, who then called the guard to deal with the matter.

Once inside, we joined the crowd on their way upstairs to the gallery. I lost Tommy in the scramble for a seat. The seat on my left was occupied by a fat lady who was busy peeling an orange. On my right was a thin-faced man with a moustache and blotchy skin. He was the one who gave a friendly smile and a cheery 'Good evening'. I nodded amiably.

'The Spanish consul is here,' he told me. Then leaning further over to me he whispered in my ear: 'Did you see that crowd of shit in the streets? After this meeting is over, our boys have been ordered to tear into them!' (An expression implying extreme violence.)

I answered: 'That's what's needed. A clean-up of all the filth, everywhere.'

Little did he know I was referring to him, to his associates, and in particular, to that alliance of the devil: Hitler and Mussolini. A plague on them all. My father would have put it in another way: '*Zol zey alamin chappen a cholera.*' Though far from the stage (the platform) my young eyes were sharp and clear, as was my hearing. The first speaker was

getting into his stride. It can be said he was addressing a captive
audience . . . of stooges. Encouraged by much applause and cheers, he
went on . . . 'and the forces of General Franco will not be halted until
complete victory is ours. It has to be made clear, to the countries of
Europe, to the countries of the East – to the whole world – that this is not
just a fight against international communism. Oh no! It goes further than
that. Our beloved general is leading a Christian crusade!'

Again, there was loud applause from every direction. But this was too
much for me. I waited until the hand-clapping and cheers had subsided,
then stood up and shouted, as loud as I could:

'Mr Speaker! You talk of Franco leading a Christian crusade. Why is
it, therefore, he is supported by thousands of Moroccan troops (Arabs)
who, by no stretch of the imagination can be called Christians? And on
the other hand, the Spanish government has the full backing of the
people – who are Catholics! The truth is being evaded by . . . '

Pandemonium. Boos for me. People were now standing. I could hear a
few cheers too.

Tommy's voice came loud and clear from the row behind: 'Good for
you, Jack!'

The voice of the speaker:

'Throw that heckler out! And don't be too gentle with him.' This was
inevitable. From all sides black-shirted stewards came at me. As the first
man neared me, he said – 'Come out quietly, and you won't get hurt.'
My neighbour, poxy-face, addressed himself to the fascist. 'I knew he
was a commie when he first came in. Knock his bloody teeth out!' I
ignored him. I was in enough trouble. But to my surprise the fat lady, on
her feet too, was beseeching the thugs: 'Please, don't hurt the boy. He's
only a kid. You have to admire someone who . . . I missed the rest of her
words, for I had become aware of the danger confronting me. Those men
were handpicked strong-arm thugs, hired for the occasion, known for
their viciousness. I then noticed one of them putting on to his fingers . . . a
knuckle-duster. Oy-oy! Am *I* in *tzorriss*! (trouble).

My memory of detail afterwards is hazy. I do recall saying – 'OK
fellows! I'll go out quietly and won't come back.' As I got to the end of
the row it seemed that a hundred hands had grabbed me . . . my body was
being assailed with blows from so many directions, whether from kicks
or punches I do not know, and with stars in front of my eyes and bells
ringing in my ears, I felt another strange sensation. It was like being in an
elevator which suddenly drops from the top of a twenty storey building

to the basement. I can't describe it otherwise. It was about then I felt as if I were on a small boat on stormy seas. Up and down... up and down. I must be mad. For I am in motion, yet I see the ground below me. Then I saw stairs. I heard a voice which seemed to come from a long distance – 'Throw the bastard down. The cops will take over...'

More horrible bumps. Then, so it seemed, an elephant stood on my stomach. I had been badly man-handled and beaten. I was turned around and frog-marched to the last flight of stairs leading to the foyer, then thrown down the last six steps. I landed near the feet of a huge policeman. I then vomited, lay still for some seconds to recover from my disorientation and looked up at the officer, standing nonchalantly with hands clasped behind his back. He was amused with a certain satisfaction on his beefy face. I made an attempt to speak. It was not my voice... more like the croaks of a bull-frog:

'Officer, I want to charge the stewards with grievous bodily harm... aggravated assault...'

Quietly he bent down and spoke: 'Take my advice, boy, get up, fuck off, and when you get outside – drop dead.' A very nice man indeed. The upholder of law and order.

I cannot remember getting to my feet. Probably the fat bastard helped me a little. And I find myself on the pavement... crowds yelling... men surging towards the entrance, trying to get in, police with truncheons swinging – then my most terrifying experience. A police-horse running towards me at speed, shouts of terror from women in the crowd; I fall down from fear and weakness – and the last thing I hear is a man shouting near me – '*Our* day will come!'

I came to in a taxi, my painful head on a woman's lap. A man's gentle voice – 'You'll be all right sonny. Just relax. We're taking you for a check-up at the Royal Infirmary.'

This was my first brush with fascism. 'Brush' was the operative word, for I had been almost swept into oblivion. At the hospital, I had to wait thirty minutes before getting attention. The emergency ward was over-flowing with casualties, mostly as a result of police assault. Apparently not bleeding to death, or considered worthy of priority, I just had to wait my turn. Still the elderly couple, a Mr and Mrs Stevenson, stayed with me. Owing to such nice folk, warm and kindly, I have never lost my faith in humanity. When I offered to pay the cost of the taxi they smiled and said:

'Don't you worry about such things. I think we can afford it more than you, sonny. We're sorry for you – and for your poor mother. Dear me, why must people be so cruel. Never mind – you're a sturdy wee fellow – you'll soon get over it.'

And they were right. Apart from a broken rib, massive bruises all over my body, and slight concussion, I was in one piece. I had head wounds and a beautiful black, discoloured eye, which was closed. My jacket was torn too, at the lapel and at the vent, and I was minus a shoe.

I was kept overnight in a ward. I did not mind this. The night-nurse was a 'smasher'. I was well looked after by her.

The kindly Stevensons had phoned one of my relations who had a telephone at home. In turn, this cousin went round to my house, and told the family to collect me in the morning.

And on that morning, with a tight bandage around my chest, and a list of instructions from the doctor (also a nice Jewish boy) on how to cope with my complaints, I sat, fully dressed in the waiting-room, wondering how mum had taken the news of my 'accident'. I was as stiff as a poker, and as red-hot with pain. Fortunately, I had no difficulty in breathing.

Sam had volunteered to pick me up at the hospital. I forced a smile on seeing him. He was furious with me.

'You stupid little bugger. Who the hell do you think you are...Tarzan? You walk into a sewer, full of rats, and expect to come out nice and clean. I'm disappointed with you. I thought you had more bloody sense.'

I had to concede the logic of this. Later, Carl scolded me in his own fashion:

'My dear boy, you have a stout heart, but a weak mind. Only an idiot would behave as you did. I compare you to a flea on an elephant's back, shouting – "unless you behave better, I shall bite you." Do you realise you cannot rationalise with the irrational!'

I was deflated, dejected, uncomfortable. Then Louis put *his* oar in.

'Next time you feel tough, and want to fight, then I'll accommodate you, in the back-yard!'

Mum, as usual, saved the day. 'Why don't you leave the poor boy alone. Can't you see he's ill. Just look at him.'

She then took me, gently as ever, into my bedroom, sat down on the bed alongside me, and stroked me, caressed me, so lovingly. Then, damn it to hell, I cried, softly. I hated myself. Thankfully my brothers were not present. Mum's overflowing compassion was the last straw.

Within three weeks I was again as fit as Carl's fiddle. Apart from a few scabs here and there and other tell-tale marks around my body my exuberance for life, living and loving, had returned. Each of my brothers had expressed an apology for their initial anger with me (which I fully understood). Love can be manifested in strange directions. It arouses all forms of passion. I knew too that if Jerry had ever behaved as I did, taking on more than he could chew, then I too would have responded in like manner.

I went to the Barrowland ballroom with my good friend Sammy Williams. I was very fond of ballroom dancing, and of other things associated with the tripping of the light-fantastic. Notably girls. Not quite with the same insatiable appetite of Sam – who made a feast from sexual intercourse. No. I was more the romantic type, being satisfied with a snack, holding the lady on a pedestal for a length of time, and coming back for another wee nibble.

Unlike me, young Williams was not interested in girls. He also was not too fond of dancing. A tall, lanky boy, bespectacled, easy-going, very good-natured, he at all times showed a loyalty and devotion for me which I reciprocated.

We 'chatted-up' two girls, bought them an ice and lemonade at the balcony-café, and by the last waltz I knew I was on target. Sammy hadn't scored. His partner had suddenly remembered her brothers were to meet her at the door and take her home (an old trick, this). But Peggy, my little doll, was more than game. Sammy, at times rather naive, wanted to remain with us, and walk me home after I parted from Peggy with perhaps a 'good-night' kiss.

At Glasgow Cross, near the famous steeple, I gave him a knowing wink, shook his hand, and advised him to go straight home (as if he would do otherwise). I intended to give him a further lesson on the facts of life, later. Such as two being company – three a crowd.

Within 10 minutes I had found a suitable love-nest at the Glasgow Green, some 200 yards from the High Court. Like a cat confronted by pigeons, or a terrier face to face with a rodent, I was ready and eager to do battle. Gone now was the sadness and discomfort of the happenings of three weeks ago. Then I had felt demasculation, indignities, loss of confidence. Now, I felt exaltation, elation – the *joie de vivre* (joy of living).

It was not, however, going to be a smooth run. And I may say that, if it were, my longing (or desire) would be affected considerably. The temperature would drop. Much of the heat would then be dissipated. A question of: you may as well have it, for 'it's on the table'. No! Anything too easy is not a conquest for, if lacking in fire, then much of the pleasure will have gone.

As we lay on my raincoat, which was spread on the grass (one must observe etiquette), we talked casually. Of Jackie Paterson's wonderful dance-band; such a lovely dance-floor; what a popular hall. Then I snuggled closer:

'Just think,' I whispered; 'If I hadn't gone dancing tonight, I would not have met you, darling.'

She replied – 'Oh! Listen to that, I'm yir darling, so soon.'

There is no answer to that. So I kissed her on the cheek. She giggled.

'Talk aboot Cary Grant . . . my, you're a fast one! Ah bet yir from the Gorbals.'

This surprised me. 'How did you know?'

'Easy. You talk posh, yir smartly dressed – ah like yir suit – and my . . . you kin certainly charm the birds aff the trees.'

I chuckled with pleasure. 'Peggy, the only bird ah want the noo (I was again reverting to the vernacular) is you.'

Thereupon I kissed her full on the lips. When she put her arms round my neck I felt nearer to the goal-post. Then she spoke, with some hesitation:

'You canny dae anything tae-night. You see . . . it's no the right time . . . whit ah mean is – that this is my bad week.'

Damn it. The menses. But I had heard of similar excuses.

'Well, darling, there's other nights. Something worth having is worth waiting for. Will you be at Barrowland next Wednesday?'

If I live to be one thousand years of age, I (and no other man) will never really fathom the female psyche. Or maybe, just maybe, what is called a woman's intuition is really based on man's transparency. They can tease so sweetly. Say 'no' when they mean 'yes' – or 'I hate you' when they mean 'I want you' and so on. On the Green that night I was ready to say I had backed a loser, and to be graceful in defeat, a gentleman to the end. I got no answer to my last question. Instead, she began to cry, reached for her handbag and took out a handkerchief, sniffed into it, looked at me sweetly, then embraced me.

We fell back to a horizontal position, kissing passionately. My hand wandered to her dress, which I raised. It then moved to her thighs – with no resistance. I placed my hand in line with her vagina, felt the delightful bulge and pulsation, and the warmth; we were both now trembling with anticipation, or lust.

Then came a man's voice, loud and clear: 'What the hell are you doing here? Eh? Up to no bloody good, that's for sure...'

We both stiffened, with alarm. For it was known that the Green, and other parts in the city, were the haunts of peeping-Toms and perverts. I could not see the fellow, but the voice had come from bushes nearby. Why did this intervention have to come when it did? Just as we were about to reach ecstatic heights.

Have you ever tried to take a bone away from a strange dog? Even the most friendly dog? You invoke the basic, primeval instincts inherent in all animals. It will snarl and snap at you. A man is no different. I shouted: 'If you don't fuck off, I'll kill you – you bastard.'

Then the man emerged. I recognised the uniform of a police constable. This was surprising. Usually, in such circumstances the officer would use his torch and catch such couples in full beam, the effect of that being more devastating. He came nearer.

'I don't like your language, laddie. I could have you for that!'

I was now cooling fast.

'I'm sorry, officer, but I thought you were a "peeper". My girl-friend and I were just making-up after a quarrel. Surely there's no harm in that!'

He nodded his head, knowingly. I reckoned him to be about forty-ish, a family man – a man of the world, so to speak. Then he smiled.

'If you are daft enough to bring such a nice wee lassie like her, to a dangerous place such as this, then you ask for trouble. A woman was murdered here just last week. During the day it's a safe enough place. But at night, it's dangerous.'

I got the message – loud and clear. The cop then said:

'Be a sensible lad. Do your winching (courting) somewhere else. I'm sure you'll enjoy it better.'

And with that, he turned and walked off. A very nice guy, I thought. What a pity they are not all like him.

I took Peggy home, to Maryhill, by tramcar. We kissed goodnight, and I again apologised to her for the fright she had. We dated for three months. Then I met another girl, an art student, who delighted in conversation as I did. We really had much more in common. We both enjoyed tennis, dancing, swimming, and good music, She was a *shiksa* too. Who the hell cared? After all, she may well have told her family and friends that I'm a nice boy – although a Jew.

It was late when I reached home, almost midnight. To my surprise the house lights were full on, and I heard the sounds of the violin coming from our big room. I knew we had visitors, for Carl seldom played for the pleasure of the family only. The strains of a Strauss waltz floated from the room: 'The Blue Danube'. I washed my hands. Then I walked towards the room just as loud applause was heard. As an encore Carl played one of my mother's favourite pieces – 'O sole mio'. I remained out, standing with my ear to the door, for Carl detested any form of interruption. He had been known to blow his top after a child in the room had passed wind, making no allowance for the age of the boy (a four-year old) and the fact of his parents being guests.

I made my entry at the end of the song. All the family were present, apart from Sam. Midnight was too early for him. Mum, Dad, Carl (the star of the evening) Louis, Etty, Jerry, Anna, my aunt Mary and her husband, Simon, and two couples I did not know. Loud cries of delight.

'Here he is, at last.'

From Dad – 'Here is my vee Cox.' This made me blush.

And Carl, pointing the bow of his fiddle at me, 'Here comes our wandering Jew, my other little brother, Izzy-Jack. Or is it Jack-easy?'

I think this play upon words fell on deaf ears. But he introduced me to his friends. One was a well-known local councillor with his wife; the other gentleman was P. J. Dollan, who became a Lord Provost of Glasgow (Mayor), with his lady. Distinguished company indeed.

My aunt Mary was petite, pretty, and very ambitious. Even when a small boy I had said to my mother: 'How can Mary be my auntie? She is so young. I want to marry her when I'm a big boy.'

She and her husband Simon (likewise ambitious) were cousins. He was the eldest son of my father's eldest sister, Bessie. The two other sisters were Gertie and Rosie. They were three small, fat ladies, and a great source of amusement to Jerry and me. They were at all times called by their Yiddish names Bashelaya, Shinageetel, and Riffka. To Jerry and me they were the Housten Sisters (who played the theatres at this period). We always referred to them as those ladies of the stage. On seeing them waddle down the street, like a mass of quivering flesh, we usually ran upstairs to warn Mum of the advancing horde. 'Ma! the Housten sisters are coming!' Mother had long since given up remonstrating with us on the need to show respect and reverence towards our aunts, her sisters-in-law. She knew that we really loved them.

They did not often visit us, for Dad called on them several times every week, being a good and generous brother. He would give them family news or the latest domestic crisis. It was appreciated that, being obese, it was not easy for them to climb the three sets of stairs leading to our house. As girls, they must have been exceedingly beautiful. All three still retained the features of their former beauty. Lovely eyes, clear, unmarked skins, small noses, and soft, pleasant voices.

When they called on us, they would always say to Mum, 'Fanny, we came to see how you are getting on, but we can only stay a few minutes.' It had never been known for them to stay less than three hours – not that Mum minded. For she would carry on with her chores and talk to them at the same time.

On the subject of my aunts, I must share with you something which still makes me smile when I think back on those days of yore, which were for us children – halcyon days.

I joined the army in March, 1940. A few days passed, then came a letter instructing me to join my unit at Enfield, London. Mum, tearfully, had asked me to visit Aunt Gertie, who was at home, dying. I duly called at her house in Thistle Street. The door was opened by my cousin Annie, who was delighted on seeing me. We kissed, then taking my hand I was led into the kitchen. The dear old lady had heard Annie shout: 'What a lovely surprise! It's Izzy-Jack!' Aunt Gertie was lying, awake, in the 'hole-in-the-wall' bed. She tried to sit up, for her visitor. The pillow was placed behind her back, to give a measure of comfort. Though very seriously ill, she was clear-headed and rational.

I joked; 'It isn't every day I have the pleasure of being in a lady's bedroom.'

I have to clarify the question of communication. At all times the old folk (the emigrants) spoke in Yiddish. Yet most of them, if not all, understood English fairly well. The reverse was with the new generation. We spoke English, and understood Yiddish fairly well. Some spoke it better than others. Anyway, I explained to Auntie, I had joined the army, and was being sent to London; and I wanted to see her, and get her blessings. With many *oy-oy*s and *oy-gevalt*s (cries of woe) she suddenly raised a forefinger, and said:

'I have just remembered something. So you're going to be all right. You won't be alone in that big place. Your cousin Philip (her eldest son) lives there too. He's doing some kind of business. Where he lives – I don't know. But he is easy to find, for he always wears a blue suit.'

As I left the house in Thistle Street, I felt sad, depressed, utterly

miserable. My aunt had about a month to live. Her two sisters had
already died. The old school, the original emigrants, were mostly gone.
This included my Dad, who had died two years before. Would my
beloved Mother survive the war years? Her death, I felt, would be the
end of my world. The sun would then be gone from earth, forever. I
could not bear her loss. I could not possibly visualise home being home
without Mother's presence. That thought brought a lump to my throat,
tears to my eyes.

I made a silent vow: 'Mum, if you will please, don't die . . . never leave
us . . . then I promise, from my heart, to be a good boy always. Never
again will I make you unhappy, cause you anxiety, or do things which
cause you upset and sleepless nights . . .' Kids were playing in this street,
as in all the streets of the Gorbals. The wee girls busy with 'peeva' and
skipping-ropes; the boys were kicking a cheap rubber ball. One little
rascal had picked up a cigarette-end, still burning (called a dog-end, or
dout) and was puffing away like a steam engine. As I passed the boy, who
could not be more than 10 years of age, he said:

'Hey mister! Gonny gie us a new fag.'

I stopped. 'A know whit ah'll gie yi – a good stiff kick up your little
arse. Smoking is bad for you – did your maw no tell yi that?'

The wee fellow looked up at me in astonishment. '*Your* maw didnae
tell *you* aboot smokin' either. You've got a fag in yir mooth . . .'

Indeed I had. I had lit up a cigarette on leaving aunt's house, without
realising it.

I did not wish to go straight home. I had much on my mind, and I
wanted to ponder over my problems, real or imaginary. Mother has to
die some day, as do all of us. It's the way of all flesh. Who would want
immortality? Certainly not Mum. For, from time to time, more so in
recent years, what with bad varicose veins, arthritis and rheumatism, and
constant pressures made worse by the bragging Nazi arch-villain Hitler
and his threats of war, she had said that death would be a relief. In fact,
when Carl or Etty would ask her to take things easy . . . to try and
relax . . . to take more rest, her answer invariably would be: 'Keender
(children) I'll have plenty of rest when I'm dead. So why should I stop
working? All I ask of you is – be good to each other.' Not till much later
did I learn mother had been a diabetic for many years.

I turned into Hospital Street, past Plotnikoff's large saw mills, then
came to Callender's bakery. The smell of bread and baigels freshly from
the ovens made me hungry. Next, I found myself passing Green's

cinema, Jacob's butcher-shop, then Gorbals Cross. This was my environment, these were my people, and soon I would be leaving all this behind. Would I ever be back? Was I destined to die in some far away theatre of war? If this be so, then may my demise be mercifully quick. As an agnostic, I feared not death. It was the dying which worried me – the thought of mutilation, agony, and being buried far from home.

But back to the main theme. The object of this true account is not war, but to give a lightning résumé of my family between the wars. Actually, this is all I can give you ... lightning flashes of highlights ... momentary glimpses of specific scenes ... mental pictures to be recorded on paper, for posterity. And let us hope that the reader, on summing-up this look into the past at the Gorbals of yester-year, may say: 'These were real people, ordinary men and women, whose passage through the Gorbals not only added colour to a drab area of this Scottish city, but whose presence may remain a lasting influence for good.' The Gorbals of today has very few Jewish folk living within its boundary. How nice it would be if someone, or some group of present Gorbalites, would erect a stone, as a symbol, or tribute to those early settlers. On it, perhaps, the few simple words: 'To the Jewish emigrants from lands across the seas. They came here, they were recognised as ordinary human beings – as we are – and were happy to settle within this area. Together, our cultures were enriched.' *Would that be asking too much?*

I have a theory. Some may scoff and say impossible ... it can never happen! This is their privilege. But I think, within the next hundred years, the rivers of blood spilt in the name of religion will have dried up for all time. How? Why? White and coloured peoples will inhabit the earth, as today, but with one essential difference. People will then not have to be burdened with the labels of friction and division. No Jews, Christians, Muslims, Hindus, or Buddhists. As Burns put it:

It's comin' yet for a' that,
That Man to Man, the world o'er
Shall brothers be for a' that.

Should this happen, then our lives, and the quality of living, will fast become Utopian. Just think of it. A man whose ancestry was Jewish would be likely to have a name as this ... Mr MacGoldberg, or Smithkovsky. His friend could be Solly Donovan, or Tom Jonesavitch.

Why not? An American general whose great-grandfather fought alongside Custer at the Little Big Horn could then be named Elmer (Bullshit) Eagle – and so on?

On the subject of strange names, let me tell you this (and I am now serious): The sweet-shop at South Portland Street, opposite our tenement, wherein most of our pocket-money was spent, was owned by a tall, bearded, orthodox Jew. His name was . . . wait for it . . . Mr Bacon. In my mind's eye I see him as he was, complete with bowler-hat and aquiline nose. He was the ideal caricature used by brainless, anti-semitic writers of fiction who were conceived in sewers. Be that as it may, the local kids gave that poor old man a helluva time. 'Mr Bacon, do you eat bacon?' Or 'One large loaf, a pound of sugar, a quarter of dolly-mixtures, and a slice of ham from your bacon.'

When we had no pennies to spend, we would stand against his window, and play at 'guessing'. Like . . . 'I see something beginning with . . . "L" ' and the other kids were to find it – it might have been Licorice-straps.

Old man Bacon was a mild, quiet-spoken gentleman. From time to time he would shoo us away from his window. On one such occasion I fell, or was I tripped, and lay on the ground nursing a bruised knee. When he came over to me I fully expected a slap on my kisser, I being the known ring-leader. Instead he bent over, looked at the sore, patted me on the head and said: 'Come into the shop and I'll give you some sweets. Will that take away the pain?'

'Oh yes, Mr Bacon, I'm sure it will.'

I now come to the most shameful escapades committed – to which I was a party. Bacon's sweet-shop and grocery was at ground level. At the right-hand side of the shop was a long dark passage, the close (or tenement entrance). There was a house, if one can call it that, on the left of the close. It had only one room, and one window, which was heavily barred, like a prison cell. This window faced the evil-smelling back-yard and a tall, dismal wall. In this room lived a family of three, Mrs Rosin, her son Joseph, and her daughter Gertie, an unfortunate trio, for all were not only terribly poor – but dumb.

That single room was unfit for human habitation. It was probably mice-ridden too, for it backed on to the shop. In those days food and health inspectors were almost unknown, and laws appertaining to hygiene and human dwellings were ever so much slacker, and casual. The Rosin 'home' was really a God-forsaken hole, for which the property-owner received a weekly rent. To be condemned to live in such squalid conditions, even in these pre-war days, was an indictment against the City Corporation.

As a boy, of course, I was not to know of such matters, such degradation, such humiliation and indignities. And again, children can be very cruel. For I helped to heap further suffering on those unfortunate people.

Mrs Rosin was small, heavily-built, and raven-haired, with piercing blue eyes. Children being what they are, she was said to be a witch. Joseph, always referred to and called Jossey Dummy, was a tall, thin, round-shouldered youth. No one could give him an age. The poor chap was always ill-looking. I suspected he had tuberculosis and asthma, at the least. He always wore an old felt hat (probably his late father's) and an old worn-out beige raincoat, and his boots were ever unlaced. A pathetic figure, to be sure.

Gertie, with blue gym dress and long black stockings, had hair and eyes like her mother. I would hazard a guess and say she would be, at the time, about six years older than I, making her about 17 years old.

A dark close, a dark eerie house with silent people inside, and confused, childish tales of evil spells and horror - all made up for the ostracism of the two Rosin children. For was not their home the Salem of the Gorbals? No one knew from where they came - nor to where they went. The hovel in which they had lived was vacated in 1930.

Although I had thrown a stink-bomb through their letter-box (I was dared to do so) and had once pulled the belt off Gertie's dress when teasing her, I do believe that I was the nearest to being a friend of Jossey's, than anyone. He let me wear his hat once, a great honour indeed. I took him to the 'Tally's' (ice-cream shop) at the corner of our street and Bedford Street - and bought him a large cone. And once I gave him a fish-cake for free. By taking my hand and giving signs, he had at one time wanted me to come to his house - an invitation no doubt to show his friendship. But I was too bloody scared to accept the offer. I was a tough kid with a long streak of yellow down my back. From the bottom of my heart, I take this opportunity of asking Joseph and Gertie, should they ever read this book, to forgive me. I would make amends if they would contact me, and would be so glad to invite them to my home, to meet my wife and children.

And now, there is more about Mr Bacon's little shop. It is an unhappy tale. The unhappiness was not for the shop, but for a lady who was employed by Mr Bacon on a part-time basis, and the lady was my aunt Mary.

I have stated earlier my aunt was a determined and ambitious woman. Ambition is a good quality, of course, but it should be tempered with reason and some patience. She was neither patient nor reasonable. If anything, she was inclined to be somewhat erratic. If she set her mind on something, then she *had* to acquire it, by hook or by crook. Simon, her husband, was dominated by her, what was colloquially known as a 'henpeck'. He lacked fire or animation but his wife more than made up for his apathy and weakness. Her interests were wide and varied. She was a one-time member of the ILP (Independent Labour Party) led by a well-known Glasgow figure, Jimmy Maxton. She was a member of a Jewish Ladies Guild, or Lodge, whose founder was an Ethel Mitchell; and a committee-member of many another local organisation. She gave much of her time and energy to everything in which she became involved. She was a hard worker, a loyal comrade, a good conversationalist, ever striving to climb higher on the social ladder, and always a loyal and devoted wife.

Mary served behind the counter at Bacon's for a few hours per week. It made a welcome change from household chores and got her into contact with customers which provided a little gossip. This in turn kept her in touch with local happenings – who was doing what, to whom, etc. And the few shillings earned was more than welcome in those hard days.

Simon worked as a tailor's presser, not a highly-paid job. So, the little money from the shop, plus about ten more shillings for part-time secretarial work, helped in augmenting her husband's small income.

From tiny acorns, mighty oaks grow. Likewise, from small, insignificant incidents, a tragedy can emerge. And this was to be poor Mary's destiny. Ethel Mitchell and her ladies were having a function, a dinner-dance, the highlight of their social calendar. As I understand it, Mary was a committee-member, entertainment section. On her shoulders, therefore, was placed a fair measure of responsibility. This she coped with admirably, having a flair for such activities. The rock on which she perished is now looming.

My mother helped in making a lovely evening dress. Etty provided the latest style in stockings, and perhaps an odd item of cheap jewellery. But what Mary wished to have, in keeping with what the other ladies wore, was a ring of such quality that it would draw looks of admiration ... such as a dazzling diamond ring. None of the females in the family could help in that direction; we were too poor for such richness. Mary, with her usual sense of urgency, concentrated on the need to be 'well-dressed'. She called on friends, far and wide, in her search for a ring of high quality, but with no success.

She travelled full circle, around Glasgow. Then she found herself at Lodge offices, where Ethel Mitchell was still working. And to the good lady Mary explained her quest ... her hope to attend the dinner fully equipped. Bingo! 'I'll lend you this, Mary, if it fits your finger.' And so it was that Mary had managed to borrow one of the most expensive 'sparklers' the Gorbals had ever seen. Our Mary was then Cinderella until the evening of the function. Or rather the mid-evening of that fateful night.

The *crème de la crème* of Glasgow society generally and Gorbalite notables in particular were present. One of the city's best orchestras was in attendance. As dinner was being served, Chopin's nocturnes and polonaises were included as a tasteful background to incessant, and sometimes inane, chatter.

Mary was so happy. Everything had gone better than expectation. The City Hall reverberated with gaiety and laughter, delightful music, wonderful food, and so many lovely and friendly people. Her euphoria had been considerably aided and abetted by the intake of some gin and orange drinks and a cocktail or two given freely to those selected few responsible for the organising of such a grand evening.

She excused herself when halfway through the meal, and made for the ladies room. A feeling of nausea had suddenly come over her. The drink, the heat, and perhaps, too, the tension of the evening necessitated a visit to the toilet. There, she vomited. After a while, when the sickness had passed, she went to the wash-hand basin to wash and freshen-up, then returned to her seat at the dinner table.

It is not known for certain at what moment of time afterwards she looked at her fingers, in order to gaze admiringly at the ring. This is not important. But when she did – she petrified in horror. The beautiful diamond ring had gone. It took her several minutes to shake off the resulting stupefaction. Then, and only then, was it realised she had taken it off when she had washed her hands. She raced back to the toilet, went directly to the wash-hand basin used by her ... it had gone! She searched everywhere. Other ladies joined in the search, but it was a waste of their time. It was too big to have fallen down the plug-hole, or so it was reckoned. She collapsed. The world had fallen on her.

I was told that the ring was valued at approximately £100. In terms of value, roughly, that sum in the 1930s was equal to around £1500 in today's money. This was a loss of the greatest magnitude. For Mary it resulted not only in domestic upheaval, leading to the beginning of the break-up of her marriage, but to her early death. In order to pay back, to compensate Ethel Mitchell, she had put herself up to her neck in debt. She borrowed money from friends, from a money-lender (a dangerous practice at any time) and also from, I think, Mr Bacon.

The poor woman had a nervous breakdown, and never returned to good health. For this, in turn, gnawed away at her mind, then she began to deteriorate in body too. She was taken to several clinics and hospitals. Consultants were consulted – a professor of neurology was called in. It was all negative. She was permanently hospitalised, lasting several years. She died in 1946 with disseminated sclerosis.

Apart from Mary's tragedy and her early demise, the Caplan family are a robust, healthy lot. If any doctor had depended on us for his living, then he would have died in penury. Though our parents had a parochial background, we, their offspring, were born free. We were never compelled to study the ancient book of Jewish law, the *Torah*. In fact, we were never compelled to do anything.

We were in accord with Jewish law in one respect: that the mother is a dominant factor, in terms of upbringing and influence; and this we can endorse. With due respect to our father, a very nice man, Mum possessed *all* the charisma. She had great wisdom. She gave us much rein to pull in any direction, but never failed to pull us up and say, in effect, 'what the hell are you up to?' or 'stop that carry-on at once!' And we did stop when she ordered.

Sam was the one fly in the ointment. Sure, he would pause and argue, then continue doing what he wanted to do. He was a rebel without a cause, a born mutineer. Alas! I was tarred with the same brush, to a certain extent. Though I jumped too when he cracked the whip, there came a time when I refused to jump as high as the others. When I left school at 14, I was beginning to feel strange urges within me – an awakening of manhood, a desire to assert myself as an adult, a different feeling towards girls, especially when they would touch me on the body. But far more worrying, there was a growing determination within me to do something about brother Sam. Even a king must die, or be overthrown, and he had had a long reign. Do not misunderstand me. I have always loved him, as I do my whole family. But I was learning to reason more profoundly. He had never brought my parents joy or pride, as Carl, or for that matter (to varying degree) my other brothers. Carl's tantrums were bad enough, but understandable due to pressures put on his shoulders. Sam was a parasite, a swash-buckler in the home, with no interest in anything but girls, drink and gambling. As it turned out, fate *had* decreed that I was to be the one who would change this unhappy state of affairs. And this was not to be until eight years later – when I was 22 years of age.

When I reached my 19th birthday, I received several nice presents from Mum, Carl, Etty and Jerry. A pen, pencil-cases, a wallet with a pound note inside, and my first watch, a pocket Ingersoll (this cost in today's money, 12½ pence). But by far the best gift was given me by a little red-haired girl, Betty, who gave me (a virgin boy) her body. She was my first love, my first experience of that wonderful thing called sex. With her, I discovered one of Life's greatest pleasures . . . sexual intercourse. She was no virgin, however. Who the hell cared? She was pretty, clean, and hot-arsed as hell itself.

I learned a lot from her. Knowing that she was likely to drop her pants, I was armed with 'tools' for my job. These were contained in a small round tin: condoms, commonly known as 'french-letters'. This was not for my protection, but for hers. For a girl to be put in the family-way in those days spelt catastrophe – nothing worse could be imagined then. I wished to play safe.

Came high-noon for me. Not at the OK corral out west, but at the entrance to a dimly lit back court down south . . . of Glasgow. At stake not my life, but the question of my manhood. Could I, or could I not 'rise' to the occasion. Would my 'John-Willie' let me down by not getting up? Will I make it or blow it? With Betty against a wall and I pressing her lips with mine, she requested me to put my tongue into her mouth 'the French way' she said.

This I did not like. I had detected a smell and taste of tobacco – and I knew she enjoyed, among other things, a furtive drag at a Woodbine. I suppose that, as I myself had not started to smoke at that period of time, it was worse for me, just like garlic eaters. If both parties had partaken of a meal containing that pungent rooted plant, then nothing would be amiss. But if only one had had it – well, it could be utter disaster.

Anyway, such kissing was not hygienic. Something not *kosher* about it. I did realise that this was simply a preliminary romp – an *hors d'oeuvre* – and I kept the forthcoming main dish in mind. My erection was now at maximum, with her hand now at my fly-buttons... when suddenly I began to tremble uncontrollably. What the hell! (I learned later this phenomenon is called a 'knee-trembler'.) I was startled by these 'shakes'. Yet, instinctively I knew it would pass. As a diversion, which would allow time for the passing of the trembling, I reached into my pocket, pulled out the tin of rubbers, and tried to open it in the dark.

Betty spoke: 'What's that you're doing, Jack?'

'I'm waiting for a bus.'

'Ha-ha! that's not funny.'

I now had the tin open, and had selected one of the frenchies. Handing it to the girl, I said:

'Put it on for me, darling, and handle with care. That's the only prick I've got.'

Her response astonished me. I had not heard such a remark before. Coming from such an attractive girl, normally so demure, the essence of femininity, it almost sounded unreal:

'You don't need one of those. This is a safe time of the month for me. You'll enjoy it better without it. You don't wash your feet with socks on, do you?'

How right she was. For she introduced me to a pleasure-land which transcended all hitherto known joys. Utterly, completely and absolutely ecstatic. My first conquest... my first woman... never-to-be-forgotten experience. Paradoxically, *not* my first love. This is called 'making love'; it is not, however, *real* love. I took her three times within the two hours spent in that passage. And when it was all over, I had formed a great attachment and respect for my penis. Now I knew it was not merely for urinating. Its other function overawed me. The wonders of nature are limitless.

Still the year of 1934. The homicidal maniac with the comic moustache, Hitler, was then one year in power. He was tearing Germany apart and already preparing for war, the Jews being his first victims. His fellow-rat, Italy's Mussolini, was likewise destroying civilisation there, and licking the boots of his Nazi masters. I was working in brother Louis's printing works. But life went on as usual in Glasgow – and the Gorbals.

I was changing rapidly from being a boy, in so many ways, to a man. I was spreading my wings . . . wanting to fly higher, and further. I was becoming restless, in a restless world. It can be said I wanted to taste other joys which were available in life before the inevitable disaster. The newspapers, the radio, the people in the streets, all talked of the drift to war. Our own politicians were incompetent, inefficient, and completely out of touch with the realities of the international situation. That was proved when Prime Minister Chamberlain returned from a meeting with Hitler and waved a piece of paper in the air, saying: 'All is well. I have here a guarantee from Adolf Hitler of peace in our time . . .' One did not have to be a political commentator or a student of politics to know that Hitler was not just a psychopath. He was an incorrigible liar too. A brick should have been wrapped in that paper and then inserted well up Chamberlain's fundamental orifice. Silly old man that he was.

Yet, on the surface, people went about their normal tasks. Things seemed so much as before. Those who had jobs worked. The unemployed stood at street corners, dejected. Buskers played in the streets; hawkers shouted their wares; women met and gossiped; kids played, as I had done when younger; and of course nothing could, or would stop Glaswegians going to a match on Saturdays, especially to a game between the 'old firms' – Rangers and Celtic – either at Hampden Park or Parkhead. Hundreds of morons (supporters of both sides) always did their best to spoil the day by singing songs that were either anti-Papal or pro-King William of Orange. A plague on them all. Bottles would be thrown; razors would flash; women and children would scream. Then the Glasgow 'bobbies' would go in and drag out the culprits. I pay tribute to our cops. They are a fine, dedicated force of men, at their best when controlling crowds and/or breaking-up gang battles; at their worst when (no doubt under orders) protecting fascists on the march. I accept it. The blame lies squarely on the shoulders of successive Home Secretaries, carrying out the policies of what were then neo-fascist Conservative governments. They were dominated by the Cliveden set — the Astors, friends of Herr Ribbentrop, the Nazi envoy to Britain.

Have you ever noticed how a tradition, specifically concerning men only, has changed since the end of the last war? Look at any photograph of men, in a group, (at work or play) and more especially a large crowd. You will find that in all such pictures before the war practically every man is wearing a cloth-cap or a hat. After the war, hardly a man can be seen with a head covering. I do not pretend to know the reason for this. It can be described as just one of these things.

I was not altogether unhappy at the Publicity Printers during those early pioneer days. The hard work was interspersed with moments of amusement. I can, for instance, recall an incident which provided interest to the customer, and much amusement for me. It happened in this way.

In common with usual practice, most printing establishments acted as agents for the large firms in the country who specialised in wedding stationery. We were no exception. For passing such orders on to them, a discount of 33⅓% was easily earned.

On one sunny afternoon, when running and feeding a platen-machine (by hand) and sweating profusely owing to the heat, the rattle of the front-door bell told me to attend the counter. Leaving the motor running, I went over to the front-shop, hopefully. Louis and Hyman were out, probably at the cinema or in some coffee-shop in town. Old Bill was downstairs checking paper-stock, and young Willie was cleaning the smaller platen. We badly needed some work in, for the 'order' file was low.

Even before I had reached the counter, the angry voices of two women came to my ears. I heard one say: 'You know whit your trouble is, maw? You think you know everything.'

The older lady replied, 'Whit you need is a damn good skelping, miss. Ah kin still gie yi one tae.'

On seeing me, who greeted them with a cheery 'Good afternoon, ladies!' I got smiles, then a question.

'You do wedding invitations here, dae yi no'?'

'Indeed we do. Can I help you in any way?'

I then brought two sample-books and placed them on the counter for their perusal. Obviously the summer heat had got at them. It can make people irritable.

'Just take your time, ladies. I'm sure you'll find what you want amongst this lot. If not, then give me a shout and I'll show you another sample book.'

So saying, I left them and went back to my work on the machine.

Several minutes passed. I had heard a few comments, such as: 'Oh! Ah like this yin...' 'Aw! That yin's awfully bonnie – whit dae you think?' Eventually, on hearing one of them shout – 'Mister!' I switched off the machine and went back to the counter. The daughter, apparently the bride-to-be, pointed to an invitation which I had guessed would be chosen. It was popular, and the cheapest in the range, nick-named by me as the 'herrie-special'. This could be interpreted as the card with most appeal to young women lacking good taste. But my lot was not to reason why, but to sell or die.

'Yes, ladies, this *is* a popular one – and very nice too.'

The mother muttered: 'That's no' ma taste, son. Ah don't like it wan bit . . .'

This remark infuriated the girl, who retorted:

'Look here maw! Who's bloody wedding is it, yours or mine, eh?'

I tried hard not to smile. Never interfere with warring women.

'Ah well. If you give me the necessary details, I'll fill in the order-form.'

As I proceeded to add names, address, venue, time and place, etc., the younger woman said: 'There's wan thing am no' too sure aboot. Whit does that RSVP mean?'

Her mother was not going to miss the opportunity of rebuking her.

'You're supposed tae be educated, eh! Well, ah kin tell yi. It's French, and it's got tae dae wi' sending a reply. Is that no' so, mister?'

Always ready for joking, I answered, 'In a way, that's right, missus. But what it really means is – Remember Send Vedding Present.' They both left the shop, laughing, arm in arm. Humour triumphs over misery.

Memories of boyhood days would not be complete without mention of some of the boys with whom we played, boys we grew up with, and who to this day remain our good friends – the life-long friends of Jerry and me.

First and foremost, the Slater brothers – Eddy and Ralph. As kids, loyal pals, as men now, they justify the respect and high esteem given them. They are two of the finest fellows ever. To have played with them then, and still to be in contact, is a great privilege and pleasure. Both are in the clothing trade.

Eddy, the older of the two, shared the good looks of Ralph, but he was by far the strongest kid I ever knew. How can I forget the day when, playing at hunch-kuddy-hunch (or some silly antics), when the object was to jump on someone's back and get a free ride along the street, it would end in pain and great discomfort for me?

I had been the 'horse' for quite a while. Lots of kids had yelled with delight as I ran up and down, whooping like a Red Indian. This became tiring, so I called a halt and suggested that Eddy, who was taller than I, should be the next horse – or did we use the word 'donkey'? I am not too sure now.

Then I thought . . . why shouldn't I be the first to grab the donkey?

After all, Eddy was the only kid who could take my weight. He was fed-up with this game, he replied, and walked away. Not to be denied my ride, I ran and jumped on his back, taking him by surprise. His reflex action was to bend and swing round violently, and I was thrown to the ground. The pain was excruciating. I was in agony. And I lay where I fell, fighting to hold back the tears which threatened to engulf me. But I dared not cry nor show any sign of weakness. Was I not the toughest kid in the whole street? My reputation was at stake. It was then that Mr Murray, on his way to work, ran to my assistance. His son John was one of our 'gang'. He was the right man, at the right moment. For he was employed by the LMS railway as a train guard, and guards were compelled to have a good knowledge of first-aid.

First he ordered me to stand up. I protested. He then bent over me, and in a gentle voice said – 'You must tell me, sonny, where is the pain coming from?' Ashen-faced, frightened, wondering too where all the peering faces had come from, I now wanted to throw up. After some moments I replied 'This arm, here' and indicated my left arm. He deftly felt along the arm. Nodded. Uttered a 'Hmm'. He followed up by saying, 'You're a lucky boy. Your arm is not broken, just dislocated at the elbow. Now! I'm going to hold that arm for you and when I tell you to stand up, you will do just that, slowly. And I don't want any nonsense from you. You're a brave wee boy. Other kids would be yelling their heads off. I promise you . . . in two minutes the pain will be gone.'

And he was absolutely right. When I got to my feet he took the injured arm in both his hands, told me to shut my eyes and start counting. I did. 'One . . . two . . .' I then felt a sudden tug . . . a concentration of sickening pain on the arm . . . then Bingo. The elbow was now back in its position. The pain was replaced by a stiffening feeling, and tremendous relief. Then the arm was placed in a sling, and I was sent home.

Other stalwarts come to mind. There was Joey Edelman, the lad who had such lovely sisters. He was a good footballer, who would have made the top in that field had he so wished. He was a wizard with a ball, having speed, stamina, and accuracy when shooting at goal. He was honest, down-to-earth, and dependable. I met him on my last visit to Glasgow recently: a jolly, likeable man today.

There was Louis Picovsky, who became a hair-stylist. Short, squat, morose.

There were the Lewis brothers, Jack and Abie. Abie was never too close to my lot, being more of a 'loner'. In no way did he shine, nor was he involved in anything memorable. But Jack, on the other hand, was outstanding. He was a star. Even as a boy he was powerfully built, and excelled in sport. We remember him most as the best diver ever to grace the Gorbals swimming pond. Trick-diving was his specialty.

Sammy Williams was my trusted lieutenant, my right-hand man. He was tall and meek-looking, but a tiger when roused. He too had several sisters. The one I admired most (in secret, of course) was Frieda. Older than I by about six years, with no outstanding attributes – yet she had that indefinable quality, that certain allure (for me, at any rate). I do not recall having 'wet-dreams', but if so, then Frieda would have been the cause. She made it hard for me.

It would seem most of my pals had nice sisters. Maybe that was the reason they were chosen to join the 'elite'.

I recall another amusing incident. On that occasion it was my little brother Jerry who shone. There was a boy called Calman (his surname I can't remember). He, Calman, was not really one of our group. He would appear, and disappear, from time to time. Perhaps his father had the kind of job which took him to many parts of the country, and possibly he took the boy with him, I do not know. Calman walked with a swagger, unusual for a lad of twelve years. This was in keeping with his nature, for he was boastful, intolerant and greedy. A dark, good-looking boy, I admit.

Everyone loved Jerry. He was a quiet, caring and loving boy, his nature being the antithesis of mine. And yet, when Calman would come on the scene Jerry would walk away. This I had noticed, but had given little thought to. For no reason I can think of, a mutual dislike had arisen.

On one Sunday morning, Jerry was sitting alone on the steps of our tenement when Calman appeared. Jerry then stood up and turned to leave, but Calman ran to him, grabbed an arm, and said, 'You don't like me, I know. Do I smell, or something . . .?'

Jerry shook his arm free. 'It's true – I don't like you! And I've got my reason for that. As for the smell . . . well, you said it. Not me. I just don't want to speak to you any more.'

I guess this was fair enough, straight talk between two kids, a clearing of the air. But young Calman was furious. He was older, bigger and possibly stronger than Jerry – and I was not around.

Touching his nose with a forefinger and pressing his conk hard against the face (thus producing a pugilistic look) he said: 'Just look at this! I do a lot of boxing — that's how I got it.'

Quietly, disdainfully, little brother touched his own nose, softly, and replied:

'You look at mine. I box also. And nobody has managed to break it. So I'm better than you.'

Calman's attempt to intimidate the smaller boy ended in failure. He was never seen again. He probably thought of my wrath to follow. But he had no reason to fear me. No harm had been done to Jerry – my wee brother and best friend.

The Big Fight

1937. Now a young man of 22 and an avid reader of the national press, I was saddened by the fast deteriorating international situation. The threat to the peace of the world came from Nazi Germany, fascist Italy, and from the Japanese who had already invaded Manchuria and were rattling their sabres at the rest of the world's nations.

The Civil War in Spain was still raging. Mussolini and Hitler were united in their determination to assure Franco's victory, whilst Britain and France were grovelling like ostriches, not wishing to face realities.

Nero of ancient Rome had played the fiddle as his city was burning. Similarly, the governments of Europe, the non-fascist states, were looking for gas leaks with a lighted match. And in the end, hell exploded, the hell which they had timidly permitted to grow to such an alarming proportion.

May the ghosts of the millions who died in the war, including the innocent victims of the Holocaust, never permit the men who brought about the conflagration to rest in peace. They deserve eternal damnation.

It soon became obvious. We were heading towards disaster. I felt this to be inevitable. The British cabinet had so many *shmucks* occupying positions of power. This is hard to believe, but true. Truthful historians will record them as having been the main instrument, or the vital tool, in the making of the Nazi war-machines.

Anyway, let us leave this aspect of pre-war intrigues, and get down to the Gorbals again. They were pulsating with life as usual. Long-bearded Jews were going into or coming out of *shul* (synagogue), accompanied by their families. The Sabbath commenced at sunset on Friday, and lasted till sunset of the Saturday. Inside, the men must wear a head-covering, either a hat or a skull-cap (*yarmulka*). The balcony was reserved for women.

The gas-lit streets now awaited the traffic and business of the evening.

Sawdust had been spread over the floors of the hundreds of pubs in the area. The smell of beer, fish and chips, and over-ripe fruit displayed on barrows filled the air. Night buskers were already playing for the long queue outside the Bedford and Coliseum cinemas. Twenty yards or so past the Coliseum, just next to Bridge Street underground station, another very old cinema stood – the E.E. This stood for Eglinton Electreum. Forever there was hustle and bustle. People were on the move, going or coming from cinemas, shops, or to the Princes theatre in Main Street. Or to the Palace cinema alongside. Younger people went to the many dance-halls in and around the Gorbals. Glasgow was the home of dancers.

It was the venue for the Big Bands, Joe Loss, Ambrose, Sid Lawrence, and so on. We had the finest halls in the country, such as the Locarno, the Playhouse, the Plaza, the West-end ballroom, Barrowland – and hundreds of side-street dives, to suit every taste.

The cheapest form of transport was the tramcar, or 'shank's pony' (walking). There were taxis, of course, but Glaswegians generally seldom used them. These plyed mainly from railway stations to hotels or designated addresses. On special occasions, such as weddings or large functions, or if a family were holiday-bound, then a taxi was hailed or hired by arrangement.

The working week was 5½ days, 9 hours per day. Glasgow was the home of ship-builders, engineers, dockers – of every craft expected in a large industrialised city. The arts too were well represented – although Edinburgh was classified as *the* cultural centre. This may be debatable.

There were ice-cream barrows aplenty, and vendors of hot chestnuts. Italians had the monopoly of this, and as far as ice-cream goes it has to be conceded, they make the best.

Glasgow was the 'second city', next to London in terms of population. On Friday and Saturday nights the streets were a mass of humanity. The south-siders (this includes the Gorbals) would either walk or take the tramcar over the Jamaica Bridge into town. They would then spread into the city's main shopping streets, Argyle Street, Buchanan Street and Sauchiehall Street. In those streets one could buy almost anything. The finest in clothing, jewellery, shoes. Top fashion houses abounded. Restaurants and tea-rooms everywhere. With many cinemas, theatres, dance-halls and clubs, not to mention the hundreds of public-houses, enjoyment was assured. All tastes were catered for.

Visiting gentlemen, or randy locals, would soon discover that the members of the 'oldest profession' were much in evidence. You would find them displaying their 'wares' in the streets between, and parallel to, Argyle and Sauchiehall Streets. Our red-light district was St. Vincent Street, West George Street, West Regent Street and Bath Street, bounded by Blythswood Square (west of the town) and West Nile Street (eastwards). Almost a square mile.

We had several good clinics too, to deal with the unfortunate gentlemen who had partaken of the questionable joys too readily, or indiscriminately. One of the best known, at the time, was Black Street V.D. centre.

From the diseased 'knob' to another type of nob. I now refer to the areas near the Gorbals wherein lived the wealthier and more elegant citizens: Pollokshields, Queen's Park, Clarkston, Giffnock and Newton Mearns, or, in the other direction, Kirklee, Botanic Gardens, and Bearsden. They would, in the main, speak English as taught at all our schools. We Gorbalites, in the main, would 'rether no' bother. We widnae want tae speak in that posh wey.'

And now, ladies and gentlemen, the main bout of the programme is going to commence. Between Sam the Terrible . . . and Jack the Terrified. Two nice boys, with too much energy.

I had been for long flexing my muscles. It could be said I was a man twice over. By the law of Moses I had attained manhood at 13 years of age – my Barmitzvah. And the law of Britain in 1937 also recognised this status, for I was six months over the age of 21 years.

Since leaving school seven years previously, at 14, the relationship between Sam and me had become increasingly strained. When he asked me to do something, I did not jump to it immediately, as in years gone by. When I did go on an errand for him, I took my time, I did not run, as before. And this he sensed. One day he grabbed me by the arm, turned me around, and said:

'Look here, Eetzky. I know you're growing up fast. You might be getting too big for your shoes. But let me tell you something! If you ever try acting the big man with me – or showing any insolence – I'll break both your legs.'

Our eyes met. I stared defiantly. He then placed a hand over my mouth and nose and pushed hard. I fell across a chair, and lay for several moments on the floor before rising, allowing time for us both to cool off.

That incident accelerated the growing animosity. The umbrage now created a perpetual simmering, or a desire for revenge. From thence on I was determined to make a stand, come what may; to end, once and for all time, Sam's dictatorial domination of the family in general, and me, in particular. And so it was. I would bide my time, and strike at the first opportunity. Sam was powerful, an experienced street-fighter, and knew all the dirty tricks and more. I was not in the same league. Perhaps the only advantage I had over him was . . . stamina. Of late he had been drinking and smoking even more heavily. His amorous exploits continued unabated. It has to be admitted I was capable of displaying a bad, vicious temper at times – and tended to minimise my own strength.

The clash came two months after the humiliation of being pushed in the face. The cause, and the end, were absolutely unexpected.

It was a Sunday afternoon on a summer day. Mum and Etty were in Queen's Park bandstand, listening to the music of a military band. I do not know where the others were. Only Dad and I were at home. I was reading a book in the kitchen, and Dad was working on a suit for a customer, in our bedroom (this was utilised as a workshop). I then heard him go into the big room. He did this when he was sewing, and required more light. He would get this from the extra large windows.

I was glad to be alone. For I had had a row with Etty, my first ever with her. It is impossible to recall the triviality which started our heated disagreement, but I believe it was due to my ridiculing Johnny. (They had married recently). And as often happens when tempers flare, things are said which are not really meant. She called me a cheeky pup. I retorted by calling her a cow – most uncalled for, I admit. In anger she said:

'I'm going to tell Sam on you. He'll sort *you* out.'

My reply to this was quick . . . 'You'll tell Sam? You've got me trembling with fear. Well, fuck you and Sam!'

The door-bell rang. I laid my book on the table and went to answer the impatient ringing. As I opened the door, it was pushed hard against me, almost bowling me over. It was Sam – in raging mood.

'You're the one I want! Come into the bedroom – I've got a wee message for you.'

This sounded ominous. 'A wee message' in Glasgow parlance could mean a punch on the nose. Coupled with his demeanour, I knew at once that we had arrived at the cross-roads. This was it. The end of a long term of servility . . . and possibly I would end up in the Victoria Infirmary, broken and battered. Well, it had to come.

I well remember the thumping of my heart . . . the familiar dryness in the throat – and a sense of the unreal. That nightmarish feeling of unreality. Reaching our bedroom he shut the door with a bang, and pushed me between the two beds. Then he took off his jacket, saying:

'I met Etty earlier. She told me you were cheeky with her. That I don't mind. But you also said nasty things about me. Say you're sorry – then I just give you a hard smack on your kisser; if not, then I'm going to teach you a lesson, once and for all time.'

Scared as I was, and with his further advantage of the element of surprise, I certainly could not, nevertheless, withdraw by offering an apology. He was not offering me an honourable retreat. Heads *I* lose – tails *he* wins.

In the distance I heard a voice (mine) saying – 'Apologise to you, *never!*' Without further ado he threw himself upon me, in the best Hollywood style. The bed collapsed, as it had done once before and we both rolled off the spring mattress. Instinctively I placed my hand under his chin to avoid the likelihood of being head-butted, and pressed upwards with all my might. He had been drinking, for he reeked of whisky, even on that Sunday. We both knew that a kick or blow on the 'balls' would end the fight, but neither was in a position to find leverage for this. My free hand had gripped his right arm. His left arm, swinging, caught me several times on the body, without effect. It was then I found myself on top of him, with his head against the gas fire. Being a warm day, of course, it was unlit. This was real drama. I remember thinking: how thankful I am, Mum is not at home to witness such a shocking display from two of her sons. I felt shame, then elation. For I knew at that moment of time, I was going to win. It was inexplicable, but true.

My right hand had continued to press. His head then was bleeding at the temple; probably it had hit the iron framed side of the bed. I then freed my left hand, reached for and touched the on/off cock, and with a quick jerk forward I managed to turn the screw, shouting jubilantly: 'I'm going to gas you, you bastard!' What melodrama! The escaping gas was now hissing. Sam began to shout: 'You little bugger! You've gone bloody mad!'

It was at this point the door opened, and Dad appeared. He took in the situation at a glance. 'Oy gevalt, keender! Voss iss doss? Oy! A cholera!'

The poor old man was in shock. He had heard the scuffle and the shouting, and come to investigate. I don't think he ever got over it. For this, I shall never forgive myself. I take it to the grave with me.

I released my pressure from his chin, slowly. I then said – 'Do we call it a day, and pack in? Or do you still want to play games?' No answer. I went on: 'It's up to you – I don't give a fuck!' Thankfully, he then replied: 'Do we call it a draw?' A facesaver for him. My better sense prevailed. 'That's OK with me.' Thus the two of us got to our feet. Dad was sitting on the other bed, shaking from his terrible experience. He was crying. And to my astonishment, Sam also cried. This I would never have believed possible. King Sam had abdicated. The Caplan household would now have a period of overdue tranquility. A happier atmosphere was born. It lasted 2½ years, until the Second World War broke out.

Simon, the husband of Mary, was an ex-soldier. He had fought at Mons and at Ypres with the Highland Light Infantry (now disbanded). He was only 16 on enlistment, but gave his age as 18. He was a complex character.

As a husband, he was quiet, morose, very much hen-pecked. Yet he too was not without ambition, being a union activist, a member of the Co-operative movement, and paradoxically a vociferous person out of doors, away from Mary's influence.

As little boys, Jerry and I were often entertained and amused by him. We would sit on his knees and he would tell us war-stories, or sing to us ballads of the day. Such as:

> When I went up the stair, I met a bobby there –
> With his whiskers tied to the railings,
> He asked me my name – said I, leave me alane!
> For my name is treacle-toffee frae the Heilands.

Our other favourite:

> Break the fire-alarm,
> Tell the butts tae flee –
> Tell the engine-man tae stop at No. 63.
> The hale o' the toon, was upside doon –
> For only a lum on fire..fire..fire . . .

He may have been a good soldier, obedient and dutiful, but he turned out to be a poor husband and father. He and Mary had three children, Sally, Gerald and Lawrence. Simon was guilty of neglecting his responsibilities. When the kids were evacuated during the war-years, Simon began to demonstrate he was a wolf in sheep's clothing. He showed little or no interest in them, the home or for Mary, just when she needed him most. This was when she was receiving regular medical treatment for nerves, and the loss of the borrowed diamond ring had aggravated her condition.

The word 'kosher' is popular with the criminal fraternity. It is used to describe something, or someone, who is sincere, clean, or above suspicion. For example, goods which have not 'fallen off a lorry', and are therefore legally obtained, are 'kosher', likewise is a man with no record on police-files. Yet, in its original context this is the name given to food which has been passed by the Jewish authorities as being clean – and fulfilling the requirements of our dietary laws. As for meat, and the recognised slaughtering of animals according to tradition, a separate authority is involved. This is the Board of Shechita.

In all matters relating to food Jews are fastidious. It matters not whether they be orthodox or not. Centuries of strict obedience and living in close proximity to one another – in ghettos – has consolidated basic, or fundamental teachings. In the old days, a Jew might be forgiven for many deviations, but let him be seen in a butcher shop which is not kosher – then it's *oy vey*! His (or her) good name has gone. His social life would evaporate swiftly. No one will wish to eat at his house. The words will spread – *'Ess neet daw.'* (Don't eat there.)

Nowadays, the strict observance to these laws has declined very much among Jews living in the west. In fact, the subject of kosher food is a source of so many jokes, told by Jews themselves, at their own expense. One of these which I remember best goes like this:

Mr Isaacstein enters a non-kosher delicatessen. He purchases some fruit, then notices a tray of freshly-cut bacon slices. So delicious-looking. So tempting. Trying to appear nonchalant, he points casually at the tray, and asks the assistant, 'How much is that, eh, that bacon?' Just at that moment comes a flash of lightning, and a terrific clap of thunder. Isaacstein pales, looks upwards, and in a trembling voice, he says: 'I'm so sorry. I was only asking.'

Talking of food which should not be eaten reminds me of a story which mother told us in later years. It concerned Sam. He was only five years of age at the time. She had to take him to a clinic, as he was suffering from tonsillitis. He was sitting on her knee in a tram-car. A fat lady sitting opposite was carrying a baby in her arms. The baby began to cry, first quietly, then loudly. The woman shook her head in annoyance, placed a hand under her blouse and out came a huge breast. Not in the slightest concerned that there were several passengers on board, she placed the tit into the baby's mouth after a slight squeeze. Sam stared, open-mouthed, in utter amazement, then turned to Mum.

'What's 'hat lady doin', mammy?'

'Shush! The lady is feeding the baby.'

A moment of silence. Sam's mystification was then apparent. Pointing a finger at the exposed breast, he shouted – 'Is the wee baby goin' to eat all that?'

It was the great Israel Zangwill who said: 'Yiddish incorporates the essence of a life which is distinctive, and unlike any other.' How very true.

For that very reason, being somewhat different in our beliefs and way of life, the Jews have suffered countless agonies by the hands of Gentiles in many parts of the world. And they, the so-called Christians, have much to answer for in the day of reckoning which they maintain must be faced, at the end.

Let me quote a few words written by the Jewish writer, I.L. Peretz:

> Yiddish, the language which will ever bear witness to the violence and murder inflicted on us, bears the marks of our expulsions from land to land; the language which absorbed the wails of the fathers, the laments of generations, the poison and bitterness of history – the language whose precious jewels are undried uncongealed Jewish tears.

In certain circumstances, particularly in conditions prevailing in a war-time situation, a man can lose everything which makes life worth living, such as his freedom, his family, any degree of influence he may have had in his community, and his dignity. What cannot be taken from him are his memories, and his train of thought. To be sure, this can be dimmed by harsh punishment, or blows to the head. In all of us, the will to live is strong, inherent. The instinct of self-preservation can supersede the blackest thoughts – or the wish to die. Jews seem to possess more than their share of tenacity to life. Does not our history prove this?

Let us forget the myths, the bunkum, if you like, of the Chosen People. I personally had appealed to God many times – had beseeched Him to give another race (the Arabs, or Russians, or Germans, in any order) that 'advantage'. For that burden has been too costly for us. Indeed, one can say with conviction, with friends like Him, who needs enemies?

My parents were immigrants from Lithuania (part of the Soviet Union) who, like thousands of other victims of anti-semitism were compelled to flee from the pogroms, the burnings, the killings, and the rapings permitted and encouraged by the corrupt Russians. Most went to America. Somehow Mum and Dad found themselves in the English port of Hull, even though their intended destination had been New York. Mum was just 13 years old, alone, frightened, disorientated. Unaccompanied, unknown, apparently unwanted. Fortunately a kindly couple on board, also immigrants, kept a parental eye on her, then guided her to a Jewish organisation in Hull who helped her to travel on to Glasgow. I understand that it was on board that train, or in Glasgow Central station, that Mum and Dad met for the first time. The good offices of a *shatran* (matchmaker) later, was instrumental in uniting them for life, as man and wife.

A large community was then being established in Glasgow, all immigrants from Russian and Polish oppression. The centre of that community was Gorbals Cross, in Glasgow's south-side. And so it came to pass that large families of Scottish Jews were formed. They found a haven of peace, a land of beauty with mountains and lakes (lochs) and a wonderful people to match – the Scots. If ever a prize will be given to a nation for its tolerance, its compassion, its humanity and understanding, and the claim to be one of the world's most civilised nations – then Scotland is assured of the presentation of gold. It is with pride that Scottish Jews can sing, 'I belong to Glasgow'.

Robert Burns symbolises Scottish attitudes towards their fellow-men by his immortal poem: 'A Man's a Man, for a' that.'

As in all things, a price has to be paid. This is, of course, a question of degree. Almost simultaneously with the convergence of Jewish refugees into the safe harbour of Glasgow's Gorbals came the influx of thousands of Irish families fleeing from the potato famine of the 1880s. It was the coming together of the Cohens and Kellys. They were different people from different cultures, and yet they blended well enough. Like the Scots themselves, our hosts, those Irish folk were easy-going, pleasant – and they liked their whisky. As a consequence to such social habits, a fight or two was no novelty. Alas! Our Irish friends brought with them a feature of living which brought much trouble to the haven of peace. This was their religious devotion . . . to Catholicism. For the Protestant Scots, this was anathema. Bigotry grew, on both sides. Although the Jew was not directly affected by these tensions, nevertheless it was unpleasant to witness such strife. Shades of the old country. Men being attacked for worshipping God in their own way. How bloody stupid! Grown men behaving like savage tribes. Whilst I condemn all religions, I still believe in the right of all people to believe in what they think is right.

If a man wishes to commit suicide, I would let him. It is his life. On condition that he leaves me alone – and takes no other life with him.

And it can be said, the friction between Protestant and Catholic developed into what later became known as gang warfare. When the industrial revolution began grinding to a stop during the '20s and the '30s, with mass unemployment in its wake, then groups of idle men, with nothing better to do, joined forces to do battle with others. Religious divisions were exacerbated by unemployment and poverty. As the old adage has it: 'the devil finds work for idle hands'.

But gang fights were magnified out of all proportion by the media. They too (notably the press) have much to answer for. To malign Glasgow and the Gorbals, of course, took public attention away from the cess-pits and corruption of London, Liverpool, Manchester, Cardiff, etc. Again, the yellow press has always focused limelight in the wrong direction, knowing that people will believe anything if it's repeated often enough. And so it was, when a Scot abroad (or in 'darkest' England) gave his address as 'Glasgow' – the reaction was typical – 'What? Oh my! I don't blame you for leaving that terrible place!'

A place where they had not even seen, except in a Sunday newspaper 'sensational' picture – which might have been captioned as 'the home of a razor-slasher'.

Apart from some half-dozen responsible national papers, the rest are trash. They specialise in glorifying someone, or something, which has reached the headlines, such as a particularly callous murderer, or mass-murderer, sex fiend or torturer; or if you're a gay, a bum-boy, or lesbian, who has had an affair with a prominent person, or celebrity – then a fortune is yours. Just tell the reporter (or ghost writer sent to you for a story) and you can become quite well off. You get perks too. TV channels will compete for the right to run a documentary on your crimes or weaknesses.

Let's put this into perspective: a diseased mind and a filthy unwashed body can spell financial success within the confines of our twisted society. The warped policy of the gutter-press needs completely overhauling. A new set of decent standards *must* be applied. When a girl whom nature has endowed with overlarge tits can exhibit these boobs, and become 'famous' – as if it were another wonder of the world . . . I ask you. What is happening to our western civilisation? I do not blame the girls, but those sick individuals who think they know how to run a newspaper. I'd tar and feather the whole bloody lot of them.

Now you may see what I mean. My reaction is a reflection of the daily violence thrown at us through the media. Violence breeds violence, just as an agitator amongst a small crowd of ordinary men can, with a little effort and some rhetoric, turn them into a bloodthirsty mob prepared to lynch the object of their imagined hatred. Let us hope that one day a form of poetic justice will be set in motion. And with a measure of justification. For I envisage an angry mob on their way to the offices of some gutter newspaper – to set ablaze the men and machines responsible for the output of so much shit.

Now for some light relief. A word of caution to the unwary traveller who finds himself at a football match in Glasgow, at any time, and more so when the game is between the maestros, Rangers and Celtic. Or as some of their moronic supporters would have it, the Protestants v. the Catholics.

Hint No. 1. *Keep your mouth shut.* Or this could be done quickly for you, by a punch, a kick, a bottle, or an empty beer-can. Or all four.

Hint No. 2. Remember, discretion is the better part of valour. If an apparently friendly fellow exhudes enthusiasm for a particular player, be sure you can identify the footballer concerned, i.e. which team he is playing for. Otherwise, when you do get home, your wife may think you have been to the dentist for a full extraction. That is, if you're lucky. It could be plastic surgery at the Royal Infirmary for a new face. Or a stitched throat.

Apart from such hazards, the Glaswegian is a damned nice chap. It is important to bear in mind the fact that only a very small proportion of fans are in the category described. But it could be your unlucky day. Furthermore, when one thinks of how a minority of Liverpool fans behaved in Belgium, causing the deaths of 34 innocent people, then by comparison, the Glasgow thug is very gentle. Or is it that our police are more efficient?

The corner-boys of the Gorbals, as elsewhere in the city, always wore caps, shirts (never with ties), and scarfs around their necks. They had the same habits, such as stamping their feet from time to time, rubbing their hands together, even though it may be a summer's day, and blowing into their clenched fists.

Any girl passing was fair game for wolf-whistles and bawdy remarks. I remember some of these exchanges: 'You've got a lovely arse, hen!' And quick as a flash, the 'lady' would answer – 'Well, stick your fuckin' nose up it.' Another time a corner-boy romeo remarked, when a girl was running by: 'Don't run, hen – you'll bile (boil) yir watter.' Once more came a speedy answer – 'Mibbe so! But you'll no' steep yir cock in it!'

To be sure, the young ladies were known as 'herries' – common specimens, and they were able to look after themselves. I can recall when a lad known as 'Rab the ram' pulled a certain young woman into a close, then pinned her against a wall, saying – 'They tell me yir a great wee ride. Well, a'm gonny fuck you...'. Her reply was – 'A cunt like you couldny fuck his granny.' Then she brought up a knee, hard, against his balls, and, as he bent in agony, butted him ever so fiercely on his nose. She then calmly walked off, leaving him almost senseless on the ground. What sweet, feminine creatures?

The Gorbals was the only area in the whole of Scotland which contained such a concentration of Jews. There were a few in Dundee, and in Edinburgh, and no doubt there still remains an odd family or so in isolation, here and there. When you consider that the Jews represented just 1% of the British population before the Second World War, it is indeed surprising how they managed to contribute so much to the country's trade, commerce and economy generally. It is even more surprising, furthermore that, in spite of having been a very small ethnic group in the UK, 60,000 Jews served in HM Forces and subsidiary units: Army, Navy, Air-Force, Merchant Navy, ambulance and fire services, etc. And several were recommended for the highest military honours, in all fronts. This was over and above the Special Jewish Battalions formed in Palestine. They assisted much in Rommel's defeat in the desert. And mention should also be made of the thousands of overseas Jews: Americans, Canadians, South Africans, Poles, Free French, etc., who rallied to the defence of our democracy, against Hitler and his fascist friends.

One should consider the fact that the Arabs, on the other hand, supported Germany, as they did likewise during the First World War. Yet, for some strange reason, the British public have poor memories in this direction. When Arab terrorists strike, as they so often do, against Jewish lives and property, it is accepted calmly as '. . .it's not *our* affair. The Arabs are simply hitting back at them.' Yet, when the Israeli Defence Force strikes at terrorist bases, the impact on the British press is like the reverberations after a nuclear explosion.

'Shameful! Jews kill women and children! Innocent Arab villagers attacked.' And so on. This would imply that Arabs only attack 'guilty' Jews. Bullshit. Just ponder, those of you who would shed crocodile tears over the judicial killing of some Arab fanatics. How would we British react to an enemy within who, during a major war, or a minor one like the Falklands, were to condemn our forces when having to kill an enemy whose task is to eliminate us?

The tragedy of war is having to kill – or be killed.

Pre-war kids of the Gorbals played with 'peerries' (spinning-tops) and 'girds' (metal or wooden hoops), set in motion and kept moving by means of a wee stick. They hired bicycles, or skates. The girls played at skipping-ropes, and peever (or hop-scotch). The lads had marbles (jorries) and of course, fitba' in the wide streets. Now and again the local bobbie caught our ball. He would put it out of use by slitting it with his pen-knife. At times he even caught one of the players. Then he would grab the 'culprit' by the ears, and threaten to take him to the station, to be hanged. Today, this would be tantamount to criminal assault charges being brought against the cop. Not so then. If we complained to our parents, then a slap on the face would be our lot. I tell you, kids of today are a different breed, more sophisticated, far more spoiled. Certainly, they are spoiled rotten, generally. And the question to be posed is this: Are they any happier? And my answer to that is a definite NO!

The mortality rate amongst children of the poor would be much higher then as compared to similar figures of current years. This is not surprising. Society has advanced considerably in terms of housing, sanitation and health-care. Medicine too has taken rapid strides forward. The diseases endemic to slum conditions have been almost eradicated in this country, thank goodness. But it has to be conceded that those who survived the rigours and deprivations of lower working-class conditions are physically really tough.

When last in Glasgow, three months ago, I met an old school-mate, whom I had not seen since leaving school, almost sixty years ago. I was in a pub on the Victoria Road, near Queen's Park, having a quiet drink alone. I sat at a table. I noted three or four customers drinking at the bar, but paid no attention to them. After some minutes, I became aware of someone standing near me. I looked up to see a short, stout man of my own age smiling at me. He spoke:

'Don't tell me . . . just let me see if I can place you . . .' (a long pause) '. . . are you the wee fellow . . . Benny Caplan?'

I smiled, stood up, gazed hard at him, then shook my head. 'Caplan *is* the name, Jack Caplan. But you've got the advantage over me, old son. I just can't remember you – and I know I should. What unit were you in?'

I had assumed him to be someone I knew in the army. We shook hands. He excused himself, went over to the counter, and came back with two large whiskies. He placed one of the glasses in front of me, sat down and spoke again:

'Ah see you don't remember me, Benny . . . I mean Jack. Well, I'll explain. You see, ah've always hid a good memory for faces. And yours hisni changed that much.' And he unfolded the mystery!

He was the little bare-footed, scraggy boy who had joined my class at Gorbals Primary, before leaving for Secondary school education. On passing the required examination he went on to Strathbungo school, and I to Adelphi Terrace, which meant that we had not the opportunity of getting to know each other better. I had felt sorry for him, pinched, pale, skinny, shoeless, and always cold. One morning I had bought two baigels (the round, crispy roll to be got at Jewish bakeries . . . the one with the hole in the middle) buttered them, and given one to him. The pleasure, the delight shown, made my gift so worth-while. I had guessed he would eat it at play-time, or would have it for his lunch. Many kids were given a penny to buy chips then, or broken biscuits from the corner-shop.

But next morning he had come over to me, and called me aside. 'My maw telt me tae thank you for that nice roll, Jacky. And we had a rerr treat wi' it. She had a wee bit o' bacon in the hoose – so we hid a sandwich between us.'

A nice, kosher roll wrapped around a rasher of bacon. I wondered what my orthodox pals would think of this. Imagine going into Geneens Kosher restaurant and asking for 'a baigel and bacon sandwich, please . . .'

But this did give me an idea for future snacks. I have had numerous such sandwiches. I can recommend it. A *maichel* (delight). I don't think I will go to Heaven. I should worry!

Well, Willie had become a master-builder after serving his time as a 'brickie'. He served throughout the war in the Navy. He came home with a little money he had saved, borrowed more, and started a business. He had retired recently as a prosperous ex-builder. His story could be repeated by other ex-slum kids. In spite of adversity, of terrible hardships, they had emerged in triumph. Courage, guts, is not a monopoly of the 'better' classes. What is more, the sense of achievement is far greater when so many obstacles have had to be surmounted. It is my contention that men who have known poverty possess a better understanding of life, have a different sense of values. They have proved themselves.

Apart from the hard core of ultra-religious families, it is true to say that Jew and Gentile mixed well in Glasgow's Gorbals. This was, to a certain extent, due to the prevailing system of the time (which may have changed; I do not know). Jewish children joined Protestant kids from the age of five, at city (corporation) schools. The Catholic schools were apart, for Catholics only.

And so, in nine years of schooling (as it was then) a Jewish boy, or girl, could have had Christian classmates throughout his or her formative years. Like so many of my contemporaries, I can look back with pride and pleasure and realise that most of my good friends are non-Jewish. In other countries, mainly in countries of the east, Jews cling together for security. This is a measure of their vulnerability. It is not so much a question of choice but of necessity. Jewish kids were always top of the class. This also left me as odd man out, for I never shone, and was not particularly bright, simply average. Unlike my own brothers, I tended to be rather slow in catching-up. But I was a plodder. I always tried to keep in the running, though never a winner.

I love the Scots. After all, I am Scottish too. They are friendly, compassionate people. My loyalty and devotion is divided equally

between Scotland and Israel. Most Scottish Jews will endorse these
sentiments, I am convinced of that. *Scotland – land of the free.*

The Italians of the Gorbals were fewer in numbers, and were certainly
more 'clannish' than were the Jews. No doubt their children had
attended Catholic schools, for I had never known any of my classmates
to be of Italian stock. But I was friendly with several of them. Their
fathers owned the ice-cream parlours and fish and chip shops. As
children, our main interest in shops were those which sold such goodies.
In the summer, ice-cream barrows appeared by the hundred in all our
streets, just as, in winter, the hot chestnut men came out in force, again,
the salesmen being 'Tallys' – Italians.

It never ceased to amuse me when speaking with Italian kids. Whereas
Jewish youngsters, in the main, were encouraged to speak proper
English, (or as my dad once put it – 'Keender, I vant you to speak der
H'English as der teacher she tells you to') and frankly, we did so – it
came so naturally to us. There was no question of affectation, or
snobbery, or of putting on airs and graces. Perhaps it had something to
do with the fact that for centuries we, as Jews, simply had always
endeavoured to apply ourselves well to any subject and to excel in all
studies. Had not our ancient scribes and philosophers told us – 'Knowledge, and the practice of it, is a gift from God. Use it wisely.' Be that as
it may, let me go back to the Italian kids.

They spoke absolutely and completely like the true Glaswegian; at
times, more so, yet nothing could hide the indefinable, foreign undercur-
rent in their speech. I put it this way. If I were to be blindfolded and told
to listen to a thousand Gorbals kids talking, and to raise my hand when
the only Italian kid spoke, I could not fail to pick out young Capaldi, or
Rossi, or Franchetti. Just as, undoubtedly, the other kids would sort out
a Jewish boy simply by the detectable 'poshness' in the voice.

And herein lies a story. It happened during the Second World War. At
the outbreak of hostilities, German and Italian civilians were interned in
special camps. This was, to a great extent, for their own safety, as
feelings ran high against such nationals. Now it so happened that prior to
the outbreak of war a young Italian man, a member of a large local
family, had been sent to Italy to visit his grandparents.

War broke out during his holiday. He was trapped. And when the
Italian fascist government got to hear of his presence, he was compelled

to join their army as an interpreter. The poor lad had no choice. Join up, or be shot.

In 1944, one of my friends, who was a sergeant in a Scottish Infantry regiment, was ordered to take a squad of his men and bring out fifty Italian prisoners from their compound, to unload ration trucks. This was in Italy, close to the Yugoslavian border. After counting-off fifty prisoners, his men began to 'shoo' them towards the waiting trucks. And of course, the Jocks had to have their fun:

'Get moving, spaghetties! If you're good you'll get big, fat ica-da-creamos. Go on, move pasta!'

Imagine their utter astonishment when, from a voice amongst the fifty Italians came this cry: 'Stick the ice-cream up yir fuckin' big, hairy arses. Yir a bunch of bam pots!' (Idiots).

It was a Scottish shout . . . a Scottish voice . . . like one could hear at a Glasgow football match on any Saturday afternoon. And it came from a prisoner. That prisoner was the young Scottish–Italian. Surprise turned to sheer delight when it was found that one of the sergeant's men had actually been at school with young Antonio.

If you visit the Gorbals today you will hear Pakistanis speak with that well-known Glesca accent. I still find it amusing. Yet why should they not? The only difference between them and the whites is colour and religion. They are Muslims, with their own temple and culture. They do not mix with their white neighbours like the Jews did, in the old days. Here and there you will see a Jew or two. And in some streets you may even see a white face. It is the Brixton of Glasgow, but instead of the predominant colour being black, it is brown.

They are a peaceful lot who mind their own businesses. They do their own thing, as they say. And I am against any form of prejudice on racial grounds. As a Jew, I can appreciate the injustice of such behaviour. For we have had far more than our share throughout the centuries.

The streets of Glasgow were ever so busy, when I was young. Always a hustle and a bustle, comings and goings of friends and neighbours; vendors shouting their wares; buskers rendering their music; women talking to each other from their tenement windows; or shouting kids, from the street, asking mothers to '. . . throw us doon a piece o' breed and jam, maw.' As often as not, instead of jam, or margarine on the bread, it was lard, for this was cheaper. I speak of the Gorbals in particular. My own territory. I knew every street and every back-court within a mile radius. I had a fight here, or felt a girl's bum there. I had pals who lived, in some cases, outside the area, some in Crosshill, Govanhill, and Mount Florida (next to Hampden football stadium). Bear in mind, when I speak of busy streets I refer not to our down-town world-famous streets such as Argyle, Sauchiehall and Buchanan Streets. Those streets are always busy, day and night. It is Glasgow's shopping pride, where you can buy almost anything, and of the best quality. No, I speak of the side streets – our playing-fields.

Those were the days when gangs of Irish navvies turned up our streets in order to make repairs to burst pipes or gas mains. No mechanical diggers then, nor pneumatic tools. All such heavy work was done by pick and shovel; by toil and sweat – in short, manpower. It was always fascinating watching those huge men work. First, they would spit on their hands, then rub the saliva well into the palm of their hands. Then they would search into their pockets for a roll of thick-black tobacco, take a bite of it, chew, then proceed to lift the cobble-stones. A pause to spit out yellow juice, nod and wink at the gaping kids, and then they carried on digging.

Many people then, men and women, used snuff. Even as a kid I thought it a filthy habit. Out would come a small tin box. With thumb and forefinger a pinch of it would be placed on the other wrist, the head would bend, sniff, sniff – then the head would be thrown back to expedite the passage of the brown powder through the nostrils and into the head proper. Usually a loud sneeze would follow, with phlegm flying all over the place.

There were bands of buskers, six days each week. On Sundays the Salvation Army came out in force to purify our souls with songs, music and prayers. They were nice, dedicated people, with some very good musicians and singers in their midst. What a waste of talent, I always thought. Mis-directed energy. As most preachers, they talk of 'pie in the sky when you die'. I'm sure they meant well. But in those pre-war days, of hunger and poverty, misery and malnutrition, surely that pie should not be in the sky – but in the bellies of so many poor people.

From time to time I read accounts in the local newspapers of rich, powerful men, tycoons, industrialists, magnates, or coal-owners, who had refused to pay their workers a reasonable, living-wage. In some cases, an increase of one penny per hour had been refused, with defiance and subsequent strikes. And yet, on approaching death, they would ask for a minister or priest to grant them complete absolution – for a price, and with proceeds to the church, of course. Therefore it mattered not whether a man had been uncharitable, or unworthy, during his life. His long list of wrong-doings were ever forgiven, on receipt of a fat cheque, with the passage to Heaven assured. Who then is the more evil of the two? The rich miser, or the hypocritical man of the cloth?

It is those same smug parasites who stand and preach morality, tell us of parables; of good, in triumph over wickedness, and to be aware of sin. Is it any wonder that the masses are turning away from religion?

I am reminded of a rabbi who had performed a circumcision on the baby son of one of my relatives. He made a nice, clean and swift job of the minor operation, no delays, no fuss, and the baby hardly cried. When the ceremony was over, and everyone was heading for the tables, which were full of rich foods and drinks, the rabbi approached the child's father with hand outstretched for his fee. The father was consumed with euphoria, with pride of parenthood; it was a notable day, a landmark in his, and his son's life. On seeing the hand in front of him, he grabbed it, shook it up and down vigorously, shouting – '*Mazeltov... mazeltov... mazeltov!*' (Congratulations). The poor cleric's face showed his disappointment. He was more concerned with payment, not *mazeltovs!*

At least it can be said that the rabbi had given a service, had done a job of work and had applied a fair measure of skill to a very important ritual in the eyes and traditions of Jews. It can also be said, he deserves a tip for cutting-off a 'tip'. The boy will grow to manhood, thankful for a sturdy, good-looking penis which cannot accumulate dirt (having no folds) and so assists the body beautiful. Judaism and hygiene go together. Again, when and if he ever becomes a soldier, he will be excused what are known as 'short-arm' inspections. Ask any Tommy what this means.

We now come to an aspect in the social lives of Gorbals children – I can embrace *all* Scottish children, for that matter – which may seem paradoxical in the face of constant, chronic poverty. House-parties.

In those days, children and adults provided their own brands of entertainment. Sans radio, television, and record-players, we always enjoyed parties to the full. It so happens, and this may sound inconsistent to younger readers, that almost fifty percent of homes had a piano, which was the pride and joy of the household. Indeed, a home with a piano was commonplace. A family would sacrifice much to possess one. New clothes, holidays, and all such expensive items would be denied in order to purchase one eventually. Strangely enough, the cost of pianos then was not prohibitive, in relation to other considered luxuries. For instance, I can never recall my home being without one, and three other households in our tenement had them.

Jewish mothers, in particular, would demand a piano even if it meant going hungry. Both parents would not mind tightening their belts further, as long as one of the children was in favour of learning to play. I was amused when, on calling on one of our neighbours, she said:

'It's so nice of you to pay us a visit, Jack. Did you know that our Abie is getting piano lessons? I think he will be another Rubenstein. He's a natural.'

I had to smile. Knowing her darling Abie, the only thing he played with was his penis. I was right. After some five lessons, he gave up. A month or so later, when playing with Duncan Murchie in the street, my sister Etty asked me to run up to the same lady, to give her some coins, being change given in an errand for her. Etty had forgotten to give her the money when she had handed over the goods. So up the stairs I ran, with Duncan at my heels. The woman's door was ajar.

I shouted – 'Hullo! It's me, Jacky Caplan! I've got some money for you.'

My alacrity was due to my optimism. Maybe she would let me keep the change. (Hope springs eternal.)

The good lady shouted back: 'Just go into the parlour. I'll be with you in a moment.'

She was attending to the call of nature, for I distinctly heard water meeting water, in the loo. So, both Duncan and I were in the parlour, standing awkwardly, near the piano. The keys were exposed, and a sheet of music was on the stand. Duncan could not refrain from tapping on the keys, as boys will do. Then came a shriek of horror from the lady of the house. We had not heard her coming.

'How dare you . . . you little hooligan! Get out of here at once. Go and break someone else's piano. OUT!'

And there you have it, in a nutshell. When little Abie tinkles the ivories, well, he shows mother that he is a promising Rubenstein, or maybe a Paderewski. But let some strange kid touch the instrument! *Oy gevalt!* A crime of the greatest magnitude has been committed. Motherly love, they call it. I commiserated with the downcast Duncan, and promised him a *latké* for free, as compensation for the humiliation given.

Now, back to the parties of yore. The highlights of the urchins' calendar. Very little excuse was ever needed for a 'gay and hearty' (party). It could be a birthday, or a Christmas/New Year fling. Or the celebration of a prize award at school, or college. It might even be, as often happened, that a family was emigrating, to Canada, the USA, or Australia. It could have been Hallowe'en. One of my friends, having had several teeth extracted, was given a treat by his mum.

'You've been such a brave boy, darling, I'm going to buy some nice cakes, some biscuits – and lots of ice-cream for you – and some of your chums. Yes, my love, you can have a party.'

Our parties were simple affairs. Up to the age of 18 or so, the boys and girls would partake of goodies (as above). The only drink consumed was tea, and lots of lemonade, Kola, Irn Bru, American cream soda. Alcoholic refreshments were almost unknown at such parties. Apart from the fact of it being dear, there was no demand for it.

By comparison to today's parties, ours was absolute innocence personified, even childish. Certainly unsophisticated, but always so very enjoyable. No louts. No drunks. No arguments. No sex either. Occasionally a couple would leave together, having met at the party, and possibly they stopped at a convenient dark spot (or back close) and had a bit of 'how's your father'. But never at the place of entertainment.

We played lots of games, some of which awarded the winner kisses. He or she would be told to 'choose the one you love, leave the room together, and kiss and cuddle.' And it would be no more than that. In truth, I usually got a 'hard-on', but always kept my little 'Willie' in check – for I was scared of being caught indecently exposed.

Those who could sing, dance, or play the piano were ever in great demand. Almost every kid had a party-piece. My forte was the telling of jokes. Many times I had been requested to give a demonstration of the tango (my favourite dance) and if any girl present was a dancer too, then we tripped the light fantastic. Shades of George Raft in Bolero. 'La Paloma', 'Jealousy'! How I loved to dance. Fred Astaire – you had a rival!

There were two girls, at that time, and I loved them both. Believe it or not, though I was then sixteen, I had no thoughts of hanky-panky. It was, I reckon, calf-love. To be near them, to touch them, was heavenly. And when they looked at me, and smiled, my heart would bounce wildly. In all sincerity, I do say this: That stage, which every boy goes through, was the most wonderful, the most fantastic period of my life. The drugs of today are supposed to give the taker a tremendous kick, to make the user float into a dream world. Yet nothing can compare to the joys of young love. When in the company of Jean Hamill, or Helen Rennie (also 16 years) I felt the real pleasure of living. This is something I cannot describe; mere words are inadequate. I only know that, for those two darlings, I would have willingly died. And ego has nothing to do with it, nor bravery, yet they caused me so much loss of sleep.

Jean had a delightful voice. Her favourite song was 'Danny Boy' (the Londonderry Air). At my request she sang, from a music-sheet, 'My Yiddishy Mama'. Helen was cute, sharp-witted, full of fun, a good talker, and a good artist. She was attending the School of Art. Of the two I think she had the edge over Jean, who was short, plump and pretty, whereas Helen was slim, shapely, and also pretty. It could well be that the reason why Helen scored on points was her coquettish manner, impish smile, and the way she threw back her head when laughing. Furthermore, she had lovely legs, and knew it. For my money, nice legs are a woman's most attractive attributes. When she sat, cross-legged, I would be hypnotised by the splendid display of her calfs and the glimpse of thighs. My imagination would run amok; my hot blood would cause me to boil-up with excitement . . . I would strip her (mentally) then feast my eyes on her nakedness, slowly, deliberately – and prepare myself for a slow climb upon her prostrate body, a hand on each breast for grip, fingers gently massaging the nipples, whilst my knee would slowly part her long legs, ready for the main, ecstatic thrust.

She knew what was going through my mind, and I knew this. This simply served to increase the tempo, to fan the fires of passion. She also knew that I was not the type of boy who would go crazy and force myself on her or rape her. The emotional rejection was hell. All my instincts, that of primitive man, were to satisfy my lust, my desires. I suppose this is the essential difference between the ape and modern man: the need to exercise control. And yet, the fact that she had the ability to rouse me so easily, to do with me as she pleased, served to consolidate my love for her.

Helen had another advantage over Jean. She was able to use many Yiddish words, in proper context.

She once said to me:

'Would you marry a *shiksha*?'

When I replied in the affirmative she posed the question: 'What would your family, especially your mother, think of it?'

A good question indeed. 'Well, let's cross that bridge when we come to it, eh.'

But she was insistent. 'Jack! I'm a virgin. No man has made love to me. And I want you very much. If we were to do it and I fell pregnant, would you stand by me?'

I became angry, probably because that was a situation which could well arise. I gave the question a little thought, then answered quietly, for she had me cornered.

'Listen, my darling. In the first place, when we will make love, I promise to be very careful. I'll use a sheath – and maybe you can arrange somehow to get a cap fitted. Marriage is ludicrous. We are both only 16 years of age. I'm earning ten shillings a week in a rubber factory – I could not even afford to keep a dog or cat on that. Give me a couple of years more, then we can talk of marriage.'

Her answer was to throw back her lovely head, and laugh. 'I had you scared, eh?'

I smiled at her. 'You certainly had.'

She was not finished with me. Boy, what a teaser she could be. 'Is it true that Jewish boys are stronger ... eh ... down there ... I mean ... the sexual organ ...'

Again I smiled. 'How would I know. We are streamlined, I suppose, built for speed and comfort, maybe. But not having had a chance to enter a penis competition I can only guess. I would back my prick against all comers.'

I did not tell her that I too was a virgin. Somehow I reckoned it to be prudent to keep her guessing. No doubt she would ask me, when I would make love with her. She was not yet finished.

'When we get married, we'll have kosher food all the time. No '*trayf*' (un-kosher food). We'll celebrate all '*yontiffs*' (holidays) and go to '*shul*' (synagogue). And if we have sons, they'll all get circumcised.'

For a sixteen-year old *shiksha*, she was sure on the ball. No flies on her. She was a very shrewd and capable young lady, far brighter than so many Jewish girls of my acquaintance, who knew nothing about the observances of our neighbours' denominations.

As for Jean, the girl with the melodious voice, she was as shy as Helen was forward. Helen the extrovert – Jean the introvert. She loved music, and was expecting to be accepted for voice-training sessions by a professional teacher. The last time we met, which was just before the outbreak of war, was at the home of her fiancé, a good friend of mine. I can still hear her sing. For my benefit she sang two numbers – 'Only a Rose' and 'If you were the only girl in the world'. And as an encore . . . it had to be, of course, they were all so fond of me, and I say this with pride, 'My Yiddishy Mama'.

Jean's husband-to-be was killed at Dunkirk, along with about a dozen Gorbals boys whom I knew very well. Four of them were Jewish lads. *I salute them.*

Jerry's type of girl differed from my conception of feminine beauty. We were chalk and cheese, in so many ways. He preferred girls to be plumpish. As he had put it: 'I go for big boobs, and a big *tochass* (arse). That way, you get far more for your money.' Yet, by no stretch of the imagination could he be termed 'randy'. He was gentle in all ways and with all people. From an early age he showed a love for children. He would spend hours with them, telling stories from his imagination. All children reciprocated his love for them. In manhood, he was the same. Children of the family, and their friends would run to him, ignoring me in the process. He was known to take as many as six kids to the annual carnival at Glasgow's Kelvin Hall, and to the circus there, with money from his own pocket. Once, when I questioned the wisdom of his time spent on children, and money spent on so many, he looked at me with his blue eyes and shook his head sadly.

'Jack, I never question you on the way you waste *your* money – on girls. You're a romantic. I can't see you getting any return from your investments. For, as Confucius would say – "Man who fucks with tongue, fucks not with penis." When I hear kids laugh, see the pleasure on their wee faces, then I am well rewarded. Can you match that?'

How right he was. His verbal arrow struck the target full on. I was guilty of boasting to him of my conquests. He was no fool. He let me rant on, but my eloquent descriptions of the joys of sex were, evidently, not believed. He was so very right. I fuck with tongue, not penis. I was humbled, and felt so small.

As the song of old put it – 'Love is a many-splendoured thing'. It is wonderful, dazzling, rapturous, in all its facets. There are so many loves, coming from so many directions. Loving IS giving. Just as the heart pumps fresh blood into all parts of the body, or as numerous tributaries run into a large river, likewise the loving of one person for another is the giving of a part of yourself to him, or her. It is a process of nature, not manipulated or designed. All forms of love coming from within. From the heart. Or if you like, from the soul.

I make no apologies for loving girls and not getting the ultimate satisfaction of full sexual intercourse, until the age of 19. For in loving them, I found a happiness, a fulfilment, and a great joy. This could be, of course, ego. But ego by itself is a veneer. When a girl to whom I was attracted gave the response which all men crave, that is, the return of affection, I was 'switched-on'. As if by magic, my whole outlook took on a brighter view of living. I was so happy. In turn, I made others happy. I wished to share my happiness with all and sundry. Life had meaning then. Problems disappeared. The sun shone, the skies were ever blue and clear. The real life of economic ills, unemployment and dangers of war seemed far distant. I wanted to live for ever.

I know now, as an old man, that this was part of growing up. For ordinary folk, life is not a sea of tranquillity. Who can deny children from poor backgrounds in particular, the innocent pleasures to be had? It is the calm before the many storms ahead. The British Empire, as great empires of the past, was built on the blood, sweat and tears of the ordinary people. It was they who paid the full price of their leaders' follies, and greed for conquests.

When I see young people walking hand-in-hand in the streets, kissing, and looking into each other's eyes, I have a momentary pang of jealousy. I then see myself as I was, and I cry inwardly for those long-lost years. Years which will not, cannot, return. Life is so very short. Always, one wonders, where have all the years gone? How little was done – how much yet *needs* to be done.

On looking back through the years, I find I have accomplished little, if anything. Sad indeed. To have lived and walked on the earth over seventy years, yet to have left not more than the average man as evidence of my existence. I have taken perhaps 35–40 women, but how many would remember me, except on a purely clinical appraisal of their own conquests?

It is said that to be a good liar one must have a good memory. I would make a very poor liar, for my memory at times leaves much to be desired. What is more, I give myself away too easily. I was a blusher. When I lied, I blushed. And when the girls saw me thus embarassed, it amused them no end. I had, as most people, many faults. I was wild, aggressive at times, a non-conformist. But happily, I could never be accused of being devious, or disloyal.

At the age of 12, I met a lovely girl in a cafe. She was sitting alone, enjoying an ice-cream. Peggy was a year older than I. It was not long before I was chatting her up. She was a really lovely bird. Her father was a doctor.

This impressed me at that time. A doctor's daughter. A bit of class here, to be sure. She hoped to become a specialist in the field of medicine. Maybe, eventually and hopefully, to go out to Africa and tend the poor people of the third world. I had to show off.

'Doctor Livingstone, I presume?'

She was on the same wave-length. 'Yes, sir! And you will be Sir Henry Stanley, of the New York Herald . . .'

I chirped 'No madam. Not the New York Herald, nor the Glasgow Herald, but the Gorbals Gazette. I'm chief reporter on a special assignment. I'm covering . . . eh . . . nice girls in town this week. And how I'd love to cover you up!'

She laughed. What a lovely sound.

I do not know what came over me. When she enquired as to what my dad did, I had no hesitation in saying – 'My dad is a master tailor. He has his own business in . . . Edinburgh. I come to Glasgow usually at week-ends, to see family and friends . . .'

Funny how one can lie so glibly at times. The blushes came when her questions became more specific.

'I'm sure I've seen you in this cafe before, with other boys. Do you live with people locally?'

'Oh yes! I have an aunt in Victoria Road.

'But that is nearly a mile away. What did you say your name is?'

'Eh . . . Caplan . . . Jack Caplan!'

Then the bombshell was dropped right on my lap. I was exposed.

'Then you must be Louis' brother. I was at school with him, and I see him quite often. He speaks a lot of you, and another little brother . . . George . . . or is it Jerry?'

Did I blush. My face was like a red, red rose. I was burning with embarrassment. What the hell could one say when caught like a rat in a trap? She must have felt sorry for me. For she leaned over, kissed me on the forehead, and said:

'Jackie, I'm going to say something – a quotation, which you should try and remember. It goes like this: "Oh what a tangled web we weave, when first we practise to deceive." '

It is no exaggeration to say the Gorbals was known throughout the world as being not a nice place in which to live. For this we have to thank the cheap gutter-press and a few dramatic writers (including a local or two) who were determined to cash in on the kind of material acceptable to non-reputable papers and publishers. Just as today certain editors will find space in their columns for 'sensational scoops'. Usually these are not sensational. Simply it is what the editor himself thinks the public wants. As for being scoops . . . yes! It was truly scooped – from the sewage pipes.

Such newspaper-men simply prostitute their profession, and reap upon themselves scorn and ridicule. I concede that some people can be fooled all the time – but the great majority of adult readers are not naive. Education is free today. So what I am writing is an attempt to show that the Gorbals of Glasgow was, in my time, as good a place to live in as any working-class area in the whole of Britain. Not as good as some, perhaps, but better than most.

It was cosmopolitan. Apart from the East End of London and a district or two in Manchester and Leeds, the Gorbals was unique. It was Scotland's 'Jew town'; the only one in the whole of Scotland. They lived in perfect harmony with a greater number of Irish families and indigenous Scots, not to mention a growing number of Italians, Chinese and Pakistanis. To my knowledge, not a single case of racial trouble was ever recorded then. The police will surely corroborate this statement.

I give you a real family, my own, not a figment from my imagination, in order to show that, in spite of conditions prevailing at the time, we were not in the least troubled by the few gangs who did inhabit the district, nor did we ever encounter serious crime or racial interference. These things occurred in the 'more civilised' south.

Overcrowding in slums was a national disgrace during the '20s and '30s – not peculiar to the Gorbals of Glasgow alone. Some of our gangsters wielded razors when warring with other mobs. This happened in Soho just as often. And I'm sure when the thugs in English cities fought it out they too would be armed with weapons just as lethal. It is a fact that English gangs were the first to use firearms, and even bombs. So, once and for all time, when the Sassenachs next think of open razors, let this be associated with . . . barber-shops.

I am endeavouring to reproduce the thoughts, the feelings, and the lives of real people; the flesh and blood, the hopes, fears and dreams of children who grew up in this maligned quarter. Some of them are yet alive, having survived poverty and deprivation, and the terrible war of 1939–1945.

Records written by officials or historians are cold and abstract. I offer you, the reader, the souls of just one family who were proud to be Gorbalites. The spirits of real people. I give you facts, not fiction or hearsay.

As a survivor of those halcyon days, and of sound mind and body, I bear witness: The Gorbals of old, of my boyhood, is dear to my heart. I mourn for those wonderful people now gone. Were I a rich man, I would present a monument, or simple plaque, to be placed in or near Gorbals Cross, and this would say, in a simple fashion:

'To commemorate the settling of Jewish immigrants from far-off lands in the east, refugees from oppression, who inhabited the Gorbals from *circa* 1895 till 1945, in great numbers. They were proud to live amongst us – and we were the richer for having them. For they were good citizens.'

If the Glasgow city fathers read this book, then perhaps such a message for posterity could materialise. Who knows? Some dreams can come true.

Jews are forbidden by their Law to ignore, or turn away, anyone who asks for help. This is surely known to many non-Jews, for beggars, down-and-outs or 'chancers' were to be seen almost daily at the doors of Jewish homes. My mother, for one, never refused help. It would be, at the very least, buttered bread, and at best, a plate of hot soup, some old clothes or shoes, and a penny or two. On this theme I have a story to tell.

Two Glasgow men had walked to Leeds, in search of work. When they arrived in that city, footsore and weary, they found shelter from the rain in a shop doorway, opposite the local office of the Board of Guardians (a Jewish charitable organisation). Incidentally, an act of charity, for the Jew, is an act of God. It is called a Divine commandment (*mitzva*).

One of the men, Big Shooey, had Jewish pals when at school, and so he was quite familiar with their way of life, in terms of whom to see and where to go when help was required in respect to food and shelter. Turning to Tam, he said:

'You wait here, wee man. A'm gonny go o'er there and have a wee word wi' the man in charge.'

So saying, he crossed the road and entered the building. He found himself in a large room, confronting a gentleman sitting at a long table.

Said the official: 'Good afternoon, sir. What can I do for you?'

Shooey cleared his throat. 'Ah've come a' the wey frae Glesca, looking for a job. And here ah um, tired, hungry – wi' no' a penny in ma pocket.'

The other stared at him, then spoke again. 'But I cannot help you. You're not Jewish!'

Shooey fidgeted uncomfortably. 'Kin ah become a Jew?'

'All right! Repeat these words after me, and then you'll be a nice Jewish man.'

And after the short initiation rite had been performed, Shooey was given twenty pounds to buy a meal or two and get him back home to Glasgow. He left the building, crossed the road, and rejoined wee Tam, counting the money. Tam was amazed.

'How did yi manage that, big yin? Yill gie me half o' it, o' course.'

Shooey looked down on the little fellow, disdainfully. 'Not on yir Nellie. *Dae you think a' we Jews are rich?*'

The above joke would imply that help would only be given to those of the Jewish faith. This is not so. It also gave the impression (though in jocular vein) that conversions are sought. Again, and most emphatically, this is not so. For the Jews never seek converts. In point of fact, for a spouse who wishes to become a Jew like his or her partner, it is exceedingly difficult. Having said that, I know of several people who changed from their religion of birth to the Jewish faith. So it is possible for people who are really sincere, and equally determined.

When the Gorbals bustled with activity during the 'Jewish occupation' the thriving population worked hard. Even during the years of depression, hard-up families were given support and sustenance from neighbours, from the Board of Guardians, and from donations sent by businessmen over and above the sums of money they gave annually to all charitable organisations. Life went on as usual. No one, to my knowledge, ever died of hunger or hypothermia. The three synagogues in the Gorbals had full congregations. These were situated in South Portland Street, Oxford Street, and Hospital Street. Glasgow's main synagogue was in Garnet Hill, off Sauchiehall Street.

The Workers Circle catered for all Jewish social activities, and sports, as did the Bar Kochba Sports & Athletic Club; and one of Scotland's finest pipe-bands was the Jewish Lads' Brigade. Other clubs abounded, such as the British Legion, masonic lodges, and several Friendly Societies. In my opinion, the gem of all was the Jewish Institute which was in my street, South Portland Street, next to the *shul*. This was, for my money, the jewel in the sun.

When I was very small, the Institute likewise was small. It was then situated in a tiny back-court in Eglinton Street. In the early thirties it had moved to 'more commodious premises' – an old church, adjoining the

synagogue at South Portland Street. It expanded rapidly, going from
strength to strength in scope and membership. I was not a member, as I
could not afford the fee. It had games rooms, libraries, a reading-room,
committee-rooms, billiards tables, table tennis, a large restaurant
(kosher, of course) and best of all, from my point of view, a large
dance-floor. A real ballroom.

The Institute, during the last war (1939–1945) had open-doors for *all*
Allied servicemen. A warm welcome was assured. It is interesting to note
that many local girls met their husbands there. It can be said romance
blossomed for the G.I. at the J.I.

Though not a member, no one was barred from entering on most days
and nights, especially on Sunday nights . . . dancing night. (I am not too
sure, but I think it did not have a licence for the sale of alcoholic
refreshments.)

I can still see, in my mind, the large cars which filled the street on that
evening, particularly. Well-dressed citizens with their fashionable ladies
entered the foyer, to be greeted by officials of the committee. Good
bands played therein. A gig at the Institute was sought after by bands
throughout the city, but I believe Louis Freeman, a well-known musician
and agent, had this all sewn-up as he was one of the city's celebrities. As
in most things, it is not what you know which counts, but who you know.

Strangely enough, I was the only one in the family who loved dancing.
Louis (that is, brother Louis) could dance – but preferred playing bridge.
Carl had not the slightest interest in it, though a musician. Sam was a
surprise to me. He was such a ladies-man, good-looking, with unlimited
patter, yet when he took the floor, very occasionally, he was like a man
with the daintiness of a drunken elephant, absolutely hopeless. Jerry did
learn to dance later. Etty seldom, if ever, went to a dance. But Anna, the
baby of the family, did dance well. Tell me, how often does a brother
dance with his sister?

As I have said, the Institute building had been a Protestant church,
whether Baptist, Methodist or Presbyterian I do not know. I do know,
however, there were two high columns at the entrance, one on each side
of the massive door. Always, on each column, a large placard was
attached. These were headed: 'wayside pulpit'. This was common then.
The message on each would be different, and would hang for a year or
two before being changed. I am assured the Irish were not involved in
one display, which stood for all to see during almost two years. On the
left-hand column passers-by could clearly read: MAKE FRIENDS

WITH YOUR WORST ENEMY. And on the other side ALCOHOLISM IS EVIL; YOUR WORST ENEMY IS DRINK. *This is absolutely true.*

There was but one shadow which fell across the paths of the Glasgow Jews. A few golf clubs in and around the city did not permit membership to Jews. These conditions were made at committee-level, no doubt, and would never appear on membership-cards or in writing, anywhere. This can be classified as being a 'Gentlemen's' agreement. Here is how I, personally, analyse this slur on the good character of most Jews who enjoy a game of golf, and I am being as objective as possible. For the record: I do not play golf, and could never afford it.

I loathe all forms of racialism, ignorance, prejudice and bigotry, whether it be Catholic against Protestant, Moslem against Hindu or any other division. Dealing specifically with a form of anti-semitism, as above, and with a wide experience of human behaviour spanning over seventy years, as boy and man, I am in a position to appreciate the under-currents which flow beneath the waters of human society, anywhere. Before proceeding further, let me tell you that in the State of Israel today there are Jews belonging to ultra-orthodox sects who believe that the Israelis, and their government, are unworthy of being called Jews. These people are, like the peoples of Iran, Iraq, Libya, and to a certain extent, Syria, whipped into a frenzy of emotion by designed propaganda. They are in every way fanatics. In short, we have Jews who are little different from other Jew-haters.

The similarity now ceases, for all those people are in no way furtive or unobtrusive – they shout their hatred for all to hear. In a sense, they could be termed as open, with the courage of their imagined convictions.

But, the 'nice, respectable' official of a British golf club who would no doubt call himself a Christian, and who would attend church services with his family, is a very different sort of fish. A 'wet' fish to be sure. I give him other deserved titles, such as a 'wimp' – a 'wally'. And definitely... 'coward'. For he wishes anonymity, to remain outwardly pleasant towards his Jewish friends, and he hides behind his colleagues, whom he has used for his own warped purposes. What would bring about such behaviour from a man who, in all other respects, seems so normal, even a jovial fellow? Why has he become so devious? Why (and I must say it) does he behave like a scurrying rat? I shall clarify.

It could be that his son is no longer top pupil at school, no longer a dux medallist, that he has been ousted by a kid in classroom and gymnasium.

And that kid is a 'Jew-boy'. I know that has happened often. This is just one reason for the wormly father to turn into a snake.

Secondly, the father could be a businessman. In competition with other firms, he has been knocked out, so to speak. The successful firm may have been Jewish controlled. That is enough. He sees the Jews as an enemy . . . the cause of his frustrations. In other words, he is a bad loser too.

It could well be that someone ran away with his wife, *and brought her back*. If that someone was Jewish (anything is possible) then the husband will hate all Jews, simply because one of them found the wife unworthy of retaining.

A kid at school once came up to me. He said: 'I don't like Jews. So I'm going to punch your big nose till it falls off.'

Now that kid didn't know any better. His parents probably set him a bad example, by their house-talk. They had possibly come out with the fable of the Jews having crucified Jesus. *As if we would do that to one of our own boys.* Anyway, that boy learned the hard way. He would never again threaten to beat-up another kid, for no good reason. He will carry the scars given him to the grave. The knife he intended using on me was 'accidentally' plunged into his own cheeks. I am convinced he will be a wiser parent than his own were.

Perhaps you had heard of the Jew who was walking past a group of navvies digging up the sidewalk. One of the men dropped his shovel, and, as the Jew got close to him, hit out and caught the poor fellow on the chin. As he lay nursing a bruised face, young Cohen looked up at the man, with pain and astonishment.

'Why did you hit me?'

'You're a Jew, aint yi?'

'I am!'

'Well, to be sure, me bhoy, you got that for moidering our Lord.'

'But that took place nearly 2,000 years ago!'

'Maybe it did and all. But I was just told that today.'

See what I mean? There is no reasoning with that sort of mentality. My late mother put it more aptly: 'A Yid bleipt a Yid. A narr bleipt a narr.' In English it means, 'A Jew remains a Jew. A fool remains a fool.'

Oh mother! If only I had your wisdom and patience. If only I were able to ignore scorn and attempts to ridicule. If only . . . I were not me. But I am me – I am what I am. How can I be someone or something else?

I have no time for fools, less time for drunks. I cannot help having a good nose for smelling out two-legged vermin. And I will not, cannot, take insults lightly.

As long as Gentile insensitivity and irrationality can erupt into the disease commonly known as anti-Semitism, then there will be friction and confrontation. Just as some men never mature into responsible human beings, likewise so many people never learn the truth of 2,000 years ago. They swallow fiction, and vomit poison, and the world suffers for their ignorance.

What the world needs is more humour, and a complete re-appraisal of biblical teaching. Better still, they should eliminate all religious crap from schools and places of worship. By all means, spread the word of God to those who wish to hear – but is not that the word of love? It is certainly not of hate. Unless, of course, Satan has triumphed, and taken over the minds of those who do not really understand the meaning of tolerance, charity or love.

I reckon I have a touch of Dave Allen's ability to scoff at religion, for I find it impossible to take it seriously, as so many do. As we approach the end of this, the 20th century, a supposedly materialistic age, there are yet too many people who believe in fairy tales.

Like the Jewish chap who asked the rabbi if he would grant him permission to bury his cat in the burial-ground. The rabbi was horrified.

'How dare you, a good Jew, request such a terrible thing. A cat in our grave-yard! Certainly not!'

The man sighed, then said: 'Then I cannot give you the £10,000 it left the synagogue in its will.'

The rabbi gasped, then reflected a moment. 'Oh! I see. Why didn't you tell me it was a Jewish cat?'

The Jews of the Gorbals lived, worked, and behaved as Jews anywhere in the Western free world. With close-knit family ties, the urge to do well at every level, from kindergarten to college, came not from a directive issued above, but from an inherent need to succeed. Living in a predominantly Christian environment, extra care was essential in order not to arouse animosity or hostility. If a Jew commits a crime, no matter how trivial, then the spotlight plays on his faith, or race. And if a Jew performs an act of charity, or does something which merits widespread praise from the whole community, then the fact of him being a Jew is somehow obscured. This has happened too often to be a mere coincidence.

Not that the Jew seeks medals or glory, or a pat on the shoulders. But like all people, he is happy with a word of praise, or encouragement as a demonstration of appreciation.

It should be remembered that the Old Testament, which Judaism gave to the world, with its Ten Commandments, is the foundation of modern justice and morality.

Any Jewish community, whether that of the Gorbals or a hamlet in Lithuania, takes pride in the honour of its members. It will never attempt to shield or condone any offence of a man, or woman, just because he or she is Jewish.

Jews, like all other creeds in Britain, are just as divided, politically, socially and otherwise. As an example, in 1939, the year of the end of my 'memories' – there were 19 Jewish Members of Parliament, almost equally divided between the main parties. They were made up as follows: eight Conservatives, six Labour, and five Liberals. This is also a tribute to the British electorate's fairness, for in most of their constituencies there were very few Jewish voters. They represented a low proportion of the total electorate.

It is not the object of this small book to list famous Jews, past and present – and just as well. For to do them justice, such a work would take several years and volumes. Furthermore, such a work would not need to include great men of the past who *might* have been of Jewish descent – as for example the painter, Rembrandt, one of the most famous in the world of art. Some of his contemporaries maintain he was Jewish and this he never denied. He painted his wife as a Jewish bride, his father as a rabbi, and went on to produce many Jewish portraits. As a great artist, he saw men and women as people, not with labels marked Jew or Gentile. He was first and foremost a humanist. Oliver Cromwell said: 'Great is my sympathy with this People whom God Chose and to whom He gave the Law.'

Another great man, Sir Austen Chamberlain, KG, MP, recorded these words:

'It is because of that hatred of persecution, which is in the blood of all my countrymen, that England stands where she does. Take that away, and what remains of the greatness, the might of the British Empire? Have we not learned that we can never reconcile people by force, never build soundly except on consent. The wider we have welcomed all, whatever their origin, the deeper has the current of our national life flown.'

And from the Rt. Hon. Walter Elliot, MP:

'Disraeli was a Jew by race and blood. A man who never drew back or apologised for either his name or nature. In these days when nations are hunting that race, let us remember that it is a mark of weakness to persecute others. Time after time the people of this country have absorbed all that foreign influence can bring, and have digested it, rising supreme above and often being all the greater for what is could absorb.'

And finally, from the late Lord Harlech:

'Wherever the Jews have been well and liberally treated they have been the most loyal and helpful members of the nation. The fundamental and only thing that holds the British Empire together is equality of status and freedom. If we were to substitute for our present conceptions of the Empire this conception of the race ascendancy of one element in it, quite frankly, it would be the end.'

All these fine sentiments expressed by great men of our recent past deserve recording, if only as a counter against constant, insidious fascist propaganda. Today (the year of 1987) there are three scourges which take a heavy toll of human lives: heart trouble, cancer (the latter not so deadly if caught in time) and the oldest disease known to man – anti-semitism. This is the easiest to contract and the most difficult to cure. Yet it is passed into the body not by germs or microbes, but by words, into the mind. It is housed in that cavity, and can then activate and multiply by stimulants, such as the hearing and the reading of, more lies. Obviously, intelligent people are not so susceptible as those who are naive and in the main uneducated. For instance, most members of the National Front are youths, yobs, and sadists. Usually they spend the week-ends attending football games, and cause violence and disruption.

Just as one cannot expect a pig to do other than grunt, so one cannot expect a dim-wit moron to think for himself. They simply do not have the capacity to do so. As a Jew would say – '*A shmuck bleipt a shmuck*' (A dope is a dope). Extreme organisations can be nullified, if monitored. This covers the far left, or far right. In point of fact, their own blatant propaganda is sufficient to warn most people of the dangers in coming too near to them. The poison which they exude is viperous. By comparison rattlesnakes are gentle creatures. I can assure the reader, we are wise to them – and so they are being kept under close scrutiny. Preferably, I'd sooner have them kept in a long, dark dungeon, under lock and key. It may yet come to this.

I have already lauded the quality of the Scots. I come back to them, because not enough has been said of their wonderful qualities. When you take away the mindless minority, such as football hooligans, it is found that the great majority of Scottish people are the salt of the earth. Let me put it this way: if the British Empire (now defunct) had been colonised by Scots alone, then I am convinced that that Empire would yet be functioning, happily. For the Scots and English are poles apart in temperament, outlook, and in their application of social and economic responsibilities. The English do tend to be rather supercilious. 'I say, old chap, after all – we're British, and all that. Are we not the pukka-sahibs of the Raj?' The attitude of a Scotsman doing the same colonial job would be – 'Ah well! we're all Jock Thamson's bairns. If you have time to bring me a cup of char, Gunga Din, then do have one yourself.' A subtle difference of approach. Psychologically, such a manner would endear us to natives, and enhance the consolidation of co-existence.

This was the way Jews, Irish and other ethnic groups were received in that land of the heather and the kilt, as brothers . . . fellow human-beings. Not as foreigners to be treated with scorn and suspicion, or as second-class citizens. I would go even further. The Union of the Crowns was good for England, but frustrating for most Scots. The English still perpetuate the myth of a Scotsman being mean, in terms of money, and again mean, in sourness of nature. Yet, nothing could be further from the truth. In so many films the Scot is depicted as the simple peasant, complete with kilt, and his vocal contributon to the story would be – 'Ach! Awa' wi' yi, mon. A'm goin' fur a wee dram.' What bullshit.

Back to the Gorbals, where men were men, and women very glad of it. Seldom have I seen the kilt worn there, in the heart of Scotland. It was sported by some Scottish Nationalists and Rover Scouts – and members of the aristocracy at their annual balls. It is all just for show. The kilt can be sexy. I actually wore it once at a function. A lady then asked me which Clan did my tartan represent. Frankly, I did not know.

I replied: 'The Clan MacGoldberg.'

'Oh! I haven't heard of them.'

If she had enquired as to what was worn under my kilt, the answer would have been:

'I can assure you, madam, that that thing under the kilt is not worn – but in perfect working condition.' (I'd be boasting again.)

Just as the Scotsman was, and is being type-cast, in English magazines, papers, movies, postcards, or anywhere else, for a cheap laugh, so was the Jew portrayed as the villainous miser (the Fagin image)... 'Oliver, I vant you to vork harder. If you steal more purses, I vill give you a nice, shining penny...' To a certain extent, both the Jew and the Scot have exploited this fallacy through the media, and many of them have the last laugh – on their way to the bank. The best comedians in the country are Scots, Irish and Jewish, and their favourite 'fall-guys' or 'stooges' are themselves.

It is interesting to note that, in his writings, Robert Burns symbolised the thoughts, the feelings and the mood of his people, the Scots. He went to great lengths in concentrating (with poem and song) on the need for brotherly love, and stressed the basic equality of men. He said that, in spite of rank or status, death was the equaliser... 'A Man's a Man for a' that'... His whole philosophy centred on real issues, down-to-earth matters, the exposure of hypocrisy – and the need to love all living creatures, even the common mouse.

Herewith is the punch-line to it, and perhaps an explanation for the synchronization of Scottish/Jewish singularity in thought, and outlook on life. It is as if one of the lost tribes of Israel had landed in Scotland many centuries before modern Jewish immigration. Let me quote from Leviticus, Ch. xix, vv. 18–34: 'Thou shalt love thy neighbour as thyself... and the stranger that sojourneth among you shall be as the one born among you, and thou shalt love him as thyself.' Which does prove Judaism first spoke and taught of the brotherhood of Man.

Possibly my light-hearted remarks, made previously, have some basis in historical fact, which would be worthy of research. There could be some validity in the MacGoldbergs and the Stewartovitches. Stranger things have been revealed in recent years. The Scots are well-known as great fighting men, excellent soldiers. Aren't we Jews grand fighters too? There is no better army in the world today than that of the State of Israel. Yes, the Jew and the Scot have much in common; they are inventors, scientists, professors, musicians, artists, writers, famous soldiers, etc. I have cause for pride in being a Scottish Jew. The highest accolade given to a brave soldier is the Victoria Cross. Jews and Scots have had their share of this much coveted medal.

A feature of Gorbals life was the presence of the 'street bookies'. It was illegal then to take monies from punters, but in general the 'polis' shut an eye on this business, and rightly so. Occasionally a raid was made here or there, as a token to the authorities of police vigilance. Usually look-outs were posted at vantage points to offset the chance of such raids being successful. In any case, even if the bookmaker was found with betting-slips and money, he was not too disheartened. He knew that (a) he could afford to pay the small fine imposed, and (b) it would be a long time before there was another such raid on his patch. The average bet was between threepence and sixpence. I knew of many poor families whose members clubbed together to raise sixpence, and who from time to time had won as much as two pounds, which was equivalent to a week's wages.

Those poor folk would share their good fortune with neighbours, even to the extent of having a party for the whole tenement. It was surprising how much food could then be bought for two pounds. Fish and chips (called fish suppers) was fourpence. Mutton pie and chips (pie suppers) were also fourpence. Tea-bread (scones) were one penny; good quality cakes from the Co-operative shops cost a penny ha'penny, or the best at twopence. Large bottles of lemonade were fourpence. And at that time there were 240 pennies to the pound (old pence). A good cinema seat was sixpence. I have taken many girls to the cinema, bought cigarettes, chocolate, and ice-cream and, after such a good evening, spent only two shillings (24 old pennies). And I was often called a 'big spender'.

There was one essential difference between Jew and Scot, in my experience. The average Jock tended to be too generous with his money (when he had some), whereas the Jewish fellow would err on the cautious side. As an example, let me mention just one venue where this can be best illustrated. A pub.

Abie and Sandy enter the pub on a busy Saturday night. The place is full of voices, some raucous – the tell-tale sign of over-imbibing; the smoke hovers thick and cloudy, and the place is bedlam. Several men shout a greeting to the pair, being acquaintances, not friends. As the two edge their way to the bar counter for service, Sandy will have taken note of the number of men who had greeted him, and on catching the bartender's eye he will order not just two drinks (for himself and Abie) but perhaps four or five extra whiskys for the others. Now this can come to a staggering amount of money – and this is just his first 'shout'! On the other hand, Abie would not be so reckless. A nod or wave of recognition would have been in order, as far as he was concerned. I do not call Abie mean. On the contrary, he is behaving sensibly, not foolishly. Very few Jews are heavy drinkers. My brother Sam was the exception to the rule.

Jews can be described as social drinkers, at functions like a wedding or a barmitzvah, or a works dinner-dance. When you think of it, it is so bloody unnecessary to throw one's hard-earned money around. For what? Just to let 'the boys' think you're a great fellow, one of the lads. Think in terms of how much food that money wasted on drink could buy, or a pair of shoes for one of the kids.

There is also the sinister side to such weekend over-indulgence. Thousands of families have been broken through drink. It is also the cause of much violence, in the street, and at home. I know countless men, normally good, hard-working chaps who, on leaving a pub absolutely inebriated and staggering home by pure instinct, become angry for no good reason, and commence to beat-up wife and children. That is the strangest part of it. Instead of being apologetic for leaving his loved ones alone (and for what?) he behaves as if he was the injured party, the innocent victim of a selfish wife.

Many of my school pals were themselves the victims of a drunken father, a lazy good-for-nothing lout, who came home on Fridays and Saturdays to beat the waiting wife and children and then jumped into bed to fornicate his battered spouse. Sad to say, this was the debit side in so many working-class Scottish homes. John Barleycorn dominated over prudence and sound reasoning. It was a curse, a national disease. I do not subscribe to the age-old excuse that it was poverty, a dreary existence, which drove men to drink. It was stupidity, the desire to be with the boys, to prove that he could drink as much as anyone.

The Irish were the heavier drinkers. Thousands of Scots also behaved abominably. I did say thousands. But bear in mind that the pre-war population of Scotland was 5,000,000, so the vast majority of Scotsmen were sober, decent and respectable. As with football thugs, the minority reflected badly on the main stream of Scottish people. It wasn't fair. Just as one bad Jew would condemn all Jews in the eyes of many. One must retain a sense of proportion, towards all things and all peoples. Common-sense should at all times prevail.

The people of the cities and all urban areas of Scotland during the long years of depression had little to comfort them. As tens of thousands of men from Glasgow particularly, and from Scotland generally, were butchered in France from 1914 to 1918, it meant that thousands of kids were growing up without a father's control and influence. Many women had to struggle alone to bring up their children. There did not exist large pay-outs or compensation as there is today, when men came home from the war minus arms and legs. The Falklands war, which was a mere skirmish by comparison to the long, drawn-out battles of the First World War, is an example of the kind of generous payments being made to ex-servicemen. Furthermore, the modern soldier is well-paid, well looked after, and serves under ideal conditions. He is no longer considered as just expendable cannon-fodder, but as a highly technical person in uniform.

How those poor women had to struggle after that first and terrible holocaust. The sacrifices made by them are too numerous to list here. And the women of the Gorbals were typical of their class, honest, hard-working, and determined to make the best of the little they had, in bringing up their children to be nice and decent citizens. It was a grim task. All the odds were against them. Yet, in the majority of cases, their children did turn out as good and respectable as those in better-off areas. In many instances, children from the slums became outstanding celebrities, including doctors, lawyers, councillors, and high civic dignitaries. At least two of them became Lord Provosts of Glasgow. Several of them were Members of Parliament. Benny Lynch was flyweight champion of the world.

There is no shame in being poor. If any blame, or shame, or stigma is to be pinned somewhere, then surely, without any doubts, this must fall squarely on the shoulders of our government and the politicians of the day. If real justice had taken place – and was seen to be done – then public hangings should have been performed in our city centre, George Square. The condemned men would be, I am sure, headed by the generals who gave the orders so often to '*recapture that bloody hill! And I don't care a damn how many soldiers we lose in doing so.*' Those god-damned generals were emissaries of the devil.

This is part explanation, a contributory factor behind the problems, and I should say the main cause of juvenile delinquency in deprived parts of any industrial city of the period.

The Scots are strongly patriotic. They love Scotland. This was evidenced on one occasion when a Jock got into conversation with an American tourist.

'Where do you come from?' enquired Jock.

'Gee, kid! Need you ask? We-ell, I sure come from God's own country.'

Jock frowned. He looked puzzled. 'I can't believe that. You've not got a Scottish accent.'

It would be fair comment to say the ruination of many men in Scotland was brought about by excess drinking. Our record as an alcohol-swilling nation is deplorable, but nevertheless true. Heart disease too has taken a huge toll; whether one is linked with the other, I do not know. It proves one thing: our national product, whisky, is fully supported as a beverage in the country of manufacture. And it is not cheaper here.

Too many English people really believe the Scot to be mean, dour, and rather simple. Nothing could be further from the truth. Such an assessment is not only the opposite of fact, it adds more fuel to the fires of contempt which yet smoulder in Scottish hearts for their English neighbours.

The Jews of the Gorbals, who lived, played and worked alongside them know better. They are kindred spirits. Both share that wonderful sense of humour, the intertwined cultures, the ability to make jokes against themselves. The stingy Scot, the mean Jew, has become a vehicle for entertaining millions of people all over the world, and the average Englishman has helped considerably to this end. As kids we used to shout: 'Sticks and stones, can break my bones – but names will never hurt me.' Indeed, the rich men of the old music-hall circuits were Scottish and Jewish comedians.

A story was told of the great Sir Harry Lauder; he was the main attraction at a Glasgow theatre at the time. He was the ideal caricature of the English conception of a Scotsman. With his kilts, and crooked stick, and songs of how to keep his pennies safe within his sporran, his songs and jokes always brought hysterical laughter to audiences wherever he played.

On one evening, between shows, he slipped out of the stage entrance, perhaps to have a 'wee dram' at the corner pub. He was stopped by a man, a poorly-dressed, hungry-looking fellow, who said:

'Mr Lauder, sir, I'm sorry to stop you, but I'm desperate. Can you give me the price of a meal, and a bed?'

Lauder's companion took the comedian's arm and attempted to brush aside the interloper. But Sir Harry pulled his arm free and turned round to look hard at the man. He was a shrewd judge of character. He realised that the fellow (who stared back without faltering) had fallen on hard times, and was not by any means the usual run-of-the-mill beggar. Something about the man's demeanour suggested a background of education, of having known far better days. Sir Harry took a five pound note from his wallet and handed it to the man, with these words:

'It's always sad to come face to face with poverty and desperation. Especially in the eyes of one so young. However, if I had smelled any sign of drink from you – you would have got nothing. Take this, and I give it to you with one condition only. *Do not tell anyone about this.*'

For, if such happenings got around, it would shatter illusions and destroy the myth of stinginess which was the background to his songs and acts. In short, here you have the true humanity underneath heather and the kilt.

When I was a boy, there were many comics on the market for children. I well remember the names of a few ... *Chips*, *Funny Wonder*, the *Wizard*, *Comic Cuts*. We were transported into other worlds: of strong men (like Tarzan) who carried elephants on their backs; of creatures who lived in a valley, and had been lost to civilisation for ten thousand years; famous outlaws and sheriffs of the American west; and of course our hero, Cowboy Charlie. But by far the most frightening was the evil Chinaman, Fu Manchu, the cause of many nightmares.

Chinamen were always depicted as slant-eyed, evil-looking hoods (thugs), members of Tongs, each with large, vicious knives up their long-sleeved silken blouses. But Doctor Fu Manchu was the arch-villain. Not only was he the brains behind the assassins, he was extremely sadistic and enjoyed torturing his victims. All his finger-nails were inches long, and sharp as the talons of an eagle. I was probably more impressionable than most of my pals. When I was about nine years of age, Etty took me to the Bedford cinema to see *The House of Fu Manchu*. She knew I was reading of him each week in my comic. Would I like to go and see him, at the pictures? This *was* a treat. I was over the moon at the thought of actually seeing him – *without him seeing me*.

Well, before the film had got half-way through, I became absolutely terrified. To my imaginative mind, all the figures sitting around me in the dark were Tong members ... silently watching me, ready to pounce and cut me to shreds. I could bear it no longer. I began to cry, jumped on Etty's lap and hid my face against her breast, for protection. In spite of her words of comfort, her soothing caresses, her kisses on my cheek, I kept crying, whimpering with fear. I now like to think that, possibly, I was as much concerned for her as I was for myself, for I loved my big sister. She was always sweet, kind and gentle.

The point is this: children are not alone in building-up wrong images of people; not alone in their inability to separate fiction from reality; not alone in jumping to wrong conclusions; not alone in swallowing lies, if they are repeated often enough. I was convinced then that all Chinamen were evil killers, just as so many grown-ups today believe that Jews and Scots are mean people, potentially wild and dangerous. Did not the Scots kill lots of English troops at Bannockburn? And were punished at Flodden Field? And the Jews! Did not they crucify our Lord? These fixations are difficult to move. Without any doubt, with regard to the latter allegation, that is the longest-lived fairy story of all times. Millions of adults still believe it.

It is well-known to modern sales directors that repetition is of vital significance. By concentration on one thing, one article (and its supposed benefits) then it will eventually be believed. It is a form of mass-hypnotism. The Christians of old were no fools. They knew this too, and long before it had become a basis for selling washing-machines. Yes sir. They have a helluva lot to answer for, centuries of blood-spilling by illiterates and morons. Fu Manchu was a boy scout compared to the 'sages' who dreamed-up that whopper. Simply blame the Jews, not the Romans under Pontius Pilate. To be sure, humans do behave like sheep. One jumps, the others jump.

In these 'enlightened' times, mountains of designed lies are called 'propaganda'. Dr Joseph Goebbels, the Nazi with the twisted limb and warped mind, was the rat in charge of the verminous-lies department of the Hitler war machine. He may have been – no, he was – utterly evil. But he was good at his job. His stories were so far-fetched, so ludicrous, so far removed from the possibility of even being remotely true; yet *he* knew they would be believed by all Nazis – because they wanted to believe them. This is the application of elementary psychology. And let's be honest about it, though it will hurt. Some of the shit which the mad Goebbels came out with was believed by prominent people in Britain, such as the Astors, of Cliveden Manor, certain members of the British government, MPs, and of course the Union of Fascists headed by that rich crank, Oswald Moseley. No denials from these quarters can alter the awful truth. For they were the people who, behind the scenes, were trying hard to encourage the British to become allies of the Nazis, against the

Russians. Whilst I have always detested the Russians for what they have done, and are still doing, to the Jews, nonetheless they were preferable to the monsters of Berlin.

Let us return to the Glasgow I love. Let me quote Alexander Smith, who wrote this poem of our beloved city:

> Draw thy fierce streams of blinding ore,
> Smite on a thousand anvils, roar
>   Down to thy harbour-bars;
> Smoulder in smoky sunsets, flare
> On rainy nights, with streets and square
>   Lie open to the stars.
> From terrace proud to alley base
> I know thee as my mother's face.
>
> When sunset bathes thee in her gold,
> In wreaths of bronze thy sides are rolled,
>   Thy smoke is dusky fire;
> And, from the glory round thee poured,
> A sunbeam like an angel's sword
>   Shivers upon a spire...
>
> All raptures of this mortal breath,
> Solemnities of Life and Death,
>   Dwell in thy noise alone:
> Of me thou hast become a part –
> Some kindred with my human heart
>   Lives in thy streets of stone...

The changes taking place in the city streets and homes, were amazing and wonderful to behold. Electric lighting on streets and houses was fast replacing the gas mantles everywhere. Old Ford cars and vans, called 'Tin Lizzies' by the kids, who were at one time able to run faster than these cars could go at top gear, were becoming obsolete. Sleeker, faster, and of course more expensive vehicles were now to be seen in growing numbers. No longer had the driver to start his engine by swinging it from the outside by means of a long starting-handle. Automatic ignition was now in vogue. I had my first driving lesson in 1935. I was twenty years of age. As I drove the old Ford out of the garage at Byres Road, I felt as proud as a peacock. Though my instructor advised me later to 'keep to bicycles, son'.

People were changing along with fashion and consumer goods; gents' suits could be bought for as little as £1.5s. Whisky was 12s.6d a bottle.

For the first time ever, Mum was able to buy a carpet for the big room. Most homes had a radio, besides a gramophone. And there was talk of something called television which, so it was rumoured, was already operating in the United States of America.

Girls were dressing more sexily. They now had nylon stockings, and were allowed to show off a bit more of their legs. Boys of sixteen stopped pissing on the edge of sidewalks; as if, suddenly, they had become aware of having a better use for their 'Willies'. The birds were not as coy as they once were, and they used cosmetics more often, and openly. I first saw, at this time in my life, girls actually smoking in the streets. Good Heavens! What was the world coming to? Women smoking in public! And I was told that in some pubs dames were being allowed in, for the very first time. A revolution, to be sure. But alas! Still not an industrial one. Unemployment was still quite bad, though slightly better than it had been.

The warmongers were busy. Armaments were being turned out fast in our arsenals – to supply fascist governments with the sinews of war. The Spanish Civil War was about to commence. The Italians were going to attack the Abyssinians, and of course the Nazis were oiling their big guns and tanks, ready for the invasion of Europe. The Japs were already killing Chinese in Manchuria. The Queen of France had said, when told that the people had no bread: 'Well, can't you give them cakes?' Similarly, our bright leaders and our rich lords of industry were thinking: 'We cannot give them all work, but the Army and the other services will find good use for them, soon.' This came true, and the 'big' boys had not been guessing.

Whereas aeroplanes had previously been an occasional sighting, now they were more numerous, and more sophisticated. They could kill more people faster with bomb and heavy machine-gun fire. The Germans and Italians were given the nod, the wink, by our war-merchants and brass-hats to go ahead and try-out all these new messengers of death on the live targets of their choice.

Brother Louis had taken me, at about this period of my life, to join with him as members of a sports and boxing club. Louis was really good. He had the makings of a good professional – strong, well-built, cool at all times, and he carried a wicked punch. He was always a calculating person. Being a wise man, he simply wished to box as a leisure sport, and to be ready to defend himself when necessary. I was not half as good as he, but more pugnacious and aggressive at all times. What I lacked in skill, I made up for in determination and tenacity. Though only 5 feet 4 inches in height, I was squat, solid, and also strong. Those qualities were to save my life later – in Japanese POW camps. But that is another story.

The writing was on the wall. The Gorbals was changing rapidly, as all things do in the course of time. Tram-cars were being gradually replaced with trolley buses. Buses were being replaced by even more modern coaches. The passing of an era was being processed. The children of the streets, like myself, were to become the fathers and mothers of children who would also play, but not under the same conditions, for streets were now for fast, modern traffic. Many of my former playmates were not destined to become fathers. They were killed in the war, on various fighting-fronts.

If someone were to ask me to list the more pleasant aspects of growing up in Glasgow, I would give, not necessarily in this order, the following experiences: the absolute friendliness and trust of my Scottish friends and their families; having the best of two worlds, i.e. a Jewish and Scottish background; the atmosphere of complete freedom and security; the knowledge that you were not looked upon as being different (as a Jew) but as a fellow citizen. To value freedom, humanity, and one's dignity, it is helpful if one has experienced the loss of all three qualities – as I had.

On a holiday, when Glasgow banks and shops closed, or even on Sundays, it was great fun going 'doon the watter'. This was going for a sail on a steamer from the Broomielaw, near the George V bridge, to Rothesay, Dunoon, or Arran, on the Firth of Clyde. We passed the shipyards of John Brown, where the mighty *Queen Mary* was built (Clydebank), went past the 'tail o' the bank' at Greenock, and into the estuary. Then one sees what is perhaps the finest scenery in the world. Rothesay, on the Isle of Bute, was where our family once spent a week's holiday. Yes, a whole week. I was given sixpence to spend. The view of the West Highland hills on high, and the delightful waters lapping around quiet, sleepy hamlets was for me the most romantic experience. I was too young for girls then, but I instinctively felt that, when I was ready for love and romance, then I would bring the maiden to those parts. And it is so near to Glasgow.

There were usually three or four musicians on board, and they played Scottish airs and dance music (there always was space to dance aboard) and wee boys were allowed to peer into the engine-room. This, for me, was something I'll never forget. For Jerry it was more interesting. He became an engineer on leaving school. His forte was pumps and valves. Later on, he taught his skills to apprentices.

When I slipped on the oily deck, and bruised my leg, a kindly officer picked me up, took me to his cabin, and after cleaning and covering the sore with a bandage, gave me a bar of chocolate and a sixpenny bit. I was tempted to fall again and claim the same reward. I was financially viable, having a total of one shilling (12 pennies), a lot of money for a kid in those days.

There were ever so many more joys for kids who knew nothing of adult problems (and there were so many). A ride on a tramcar, 10 miles for about one penny; and the penny matinees after school hours, 4.30 till 6 p.m. We followed the many adventures of Tom Mix and Buck Jones with keen excitement; we even felt the arrows sticking into our backs when the Indians attacked the covered-wagons; and when they scalped their victims, we squirmed with fear and wonder. Of course, the Fifth Cavalry always arrived on time to prevent a massacre.

We laughed at Charlie Chaplin, Harold Lloyd, Buster Keaton, and countless other funny men. Regretfully, childhood is of short duration. Too soon our carefree days would end. On leaving school at 14 we would then become part of the adult and troublesome world. And brother, it was a rotten world.

The Scots are energetic, inventive, and always good at their jobs. You will find them all over the world, wherever ships sail, as engineers and officers; you will find them where no ships can reach, in overseas factories, jungle stations, on top of mountains, and below the seven seas as divers and treasure-hunters. They are executives and administrators; policemen, soldiers and sportsmen. You just name it, and a Scottish person will answer. The Jew is also like the Scarlet Pimpernel – here, there, everywhere. If you find a place without a Scot or Jew, then that place is not worth being in, usually.

Let me tell you of just two incidents which are not connected with the theme of my Gorbals story, but which emphasise the point I am making. The scene is a camp for Allied prisoners-of-war, in Saigon (now Vietnam). The atomic bombs had recently been dropped over Hiroshima and Nagasaki, and the Japanese had accepted unconditional surrender. But pockets of Japanese soldiers, fanatical die-hards, wanted to massacre all prisoners. The position was, to say the least, most delicate and dangerous.

The River camp was crammed with POW survivors. We did not know it then, but the Japanese general in charge of the Saigon area was at a meeting with his staff. The only item on the agenda was: 'Do we, or do we not, execute all prisoners? Tokyo has instructed us to deal with the matter as we see fit. Would the killing of those who are left make any difference to our own fate?'

As this meeting was in progress, we heard the sound of a lone aircraft. Suddenly a man shouted – 'Look! A parachutist! Just one man!' We could hardly believe our eyes. Who was he? Friend or foe? About ten minutes later another shout went up – 'There's a man walking towards the camp!' As the man came nearer we made a rush towards the gate. It has to be remembered that the Japanese guard (consisting of 12 men) were sitting at the guard-house, next to that gate, their rifles between their legs. They made no move. Perhaps they could not cope with the turn of events. And then we recognised the man as being white, in the uniform of the Royal Air Force, a revolver holster at his side. He was small and fair. A Korean guard rushed out, opened the gate, and bowed to the stranger. I was the first to speak to the officer.

'Is the war really over, sir? Leaflets were dropped this morning, saying it's all over. But we still cannot believe it.'

He looked at me, then the others. He shook his head with pity for us, then spoke.

'The war is over for you poor bastards. That's official! And I'm here to deal with the officer in charge of this shit-house.'

The officer was a Scotsman, from Edinburgh. He dropped out of the eastern sky – a welcome messenger from the civilised world. Most of us cried, unashamedly. We were going to be free men again . . .

Anecdote No. 2: We then poured out of the camp, into Saigon city. The guards made no attempt to stop the flood of near-hysterical men. British and Australians, Scots, Welsh, Irish, and two Jews, myself and a Manchester man whose name was Joe Cohen. Joe was, in many ways, a strange character, from Rumanian stock, tall, fair, and very orthodox. Our outlooks were totally at variance. We were the only surviving Jews in that particular camp. If my memory serves me right, Joe and I had covered our heads when the third surviving Jew died, and we *davened* (prayed) over the grave, facing east. I don't think this gave any comfort to the dead man, but for sure, it would do him no harm. Joe was pleased to be able to conduct the service, for I couldn't.

And so it was, we found ourselves in a busy part of Saigon. How strange it was to see white people going about their everyday business, unmolested by the Japanese. They were French. When the invading Japs over-ran their country 3½ years earlier, they imprisoned all French troops, but permitted the civilians to 'carry on as usual'. On condition, of course, they accepted the new laws imposed by the Imperial Japanese Army.

Anyway, can you imagine the scene? Hundreds of near-naked men walking around (in awe and wonder) the streets of Saigon – the Paris of the East. Shops full of goodies, motor cars passing (and rickshaws); it was so like a dream.

Then it happened. As Joe and I neared a corner, a group of white girls almost bumped into us. When they saw us more clearly, they suddenly burst out laughing. Can you blame them? Certainly not! Two naked, bearded white men, thin and emaciated, with three-and-a-half years of jungle dirt caked on them. What was more, my testicles were dangling out of my G-string, without my knowing. When I looked down, and realised why they were laughing, I almost fainted with embarrassment. They had come out for lunch, no doubt, but had not expected to run into a pair of swinging balls.

So we ran like hell. Anywhere, as long as we got far away from the laughing females. Believe me, as a man I was no good to any woman then. None of us were. We were ill, listless, and so many died before reaching home in England. We craved food, rest – and to meet death in peace.

We ran till we came to a big door with the sign above – 'Club Colonial Français'. We entered. We found ourselves in a large room, with a few score French men and women sitting at tables, talking and drinking. As they saw us, they stopped talking. The sudden silence was frightening. We were about to turn and run away when they stampeded towards us in a mad rush, shouting: 'Les prisonniers anglais!' Within seconds people were offering us drinks, cakes, sandwiches, cigarettes. We did not trust ourselves to speak, otherwise we would have burst into tears, tears of joy, relief and disbelief.

A large woman made her way to us, and began to shout at her compatriots. For a moment I thought she may have been pro-Japanese, but no! She spoke to us afterwards, in English and said she had warned her friends not to give us alcoholic drinks, as this would kill us in our present state. She was a nurse, she said, and we had suffered too much already. We were given the cakes and lovely bread sandwiches, then they left us alone to eat in peace. They understood our emotions. Bless them. As we ate, quietly, I noticed a man opposite looking at us intently. Each time I turned in his direction, he was still staring. It was becoming a little uncomfortable. Then he spoke to us. In French.

'Vous comprenez le français?' (Do you understand French?)

In my poor French I replied: 'Je regrette, monsieur.'

He thought for a moment, and spoke again. 'Quel est votre nom?'

I answered: 'Jack . . . Jack Caplan.'

The man showed surprise, and some excitement: 'Caplan? Vous êtes Juif?'

I at once caught the full significance of his stares, his thinking, and said: 'Oui! Oui!'

He smiled – then spoke in Yiddish! I answered likewise in my mother-tongue. The rapport, the affinity, had now been firmly cemented. A fellow Jew had been found in, of all places, the Japanese occupied city of Saigon, in August 1945. He was of Polish origin, and a naturalised Frenchman. I thought this incredible. Just as he felt. To meet two British soldier-prisoners who were also Jews. Of the thousands of prisoners running around Saigon, we were the ones destined to meet him – the only French Jew in the city.

I have given you, the reader, a rapid review, albeit much condensed, of my boyhood and young manhood in the city of my birth, Glasgow. I have spoken of the love I have for my Scottish friends, and for Scotland as a whole. And I am sure I speak for the many thousands of my *landsmen* (other Jews from the Gorbals) who also hold the Scots in high esteem.

If I were to philosophise on men, women and attitudes, I would put it this way: Men can endure poverty – not insults. Women can endure pain – not scorn. The staying-power, or tenacity, of the Jew, should never be under-estimated. They are tough, yet sentimental. As friends, they are extremely loyal, as are the Scots. They are not easily intimidated. Remember, when the going gets tough – the tough get going. Right is Might, and for that reason, in spite of losses, the Jew *will* win in the end.

As I see babies come into the world, watch them grow up and accumulate so much more knowledge than was possible in my generation, I feel a certain sadness. Why is there so much hate in our world? Should we not endeavour to make their passage through life smoother and easier, with understanding and compassion, no matter their colour or creed? Should we not show them the meaning of caring and loving as opposed to hate, spite and resentment? If we can do that, then this will indeed be a wonderful world.

Epilogue

On a day in March 1940, Jack Caplan walked out of his work-place and boarded a tram which took him to the Dumbarton Road Army recruitment centre. He then volunteered for service with the Royal Corps of Signals, and as Signalman Caplan, J., army number 2591725 became a driver/despatch-rider.

On February 15th 1942, he was captured with the remnants of the British 18th Division at Singapore. In the hands of the ruthless Japanese 7,000 of his comrades died within the first year – in the construction of the infamous bridge on the Kwai and Railway of Death, in Thailand.

Jack survived this and other projects built by Allied prisoners in the slave-labour camps of the jungle. As an explanation for his survival he put it this way: 'I was determined not to give those *mamzers* (bastards) the satisfaction of my death. More important, my will to live was strong. Thoughts of my mother and family, in their grief, never left me. It has nothing to do with courage – on the contrary, if I had been a good runner and got to the docks in time on February 15th '42, I would have escaped, or finished up in the belly of a shark. Simply a question of mind over matter. I was, like all prisoners, emaciated in body, but kept my mind alive with the knowledge that the war could not last forever. I JUST HAD TO LIVE, for mother's sake. Though it must be said – during the long 3½ years of captivity there were times when I felt death preferable to the sufferings of incarceration.'

Jack came home in August 1945, shortly after the dropping of the two atomic bombs which ended the war, and the horrors inflicted upon the prisoners of Japan. He was now a confirmed agnostic. To talk of the existence of a deity brings a cynical smile to his face. More so, with the Holocaust in mind. The cold-blooded murders of millions of European Jews.

Happily married today, with four grown children and three grand-children, he visits his beloved Gorbals often. For him it is a walk down memory-lane, even though many of those lanes (and streets) have long since gone. Along with so many friends and relations.

The Caplan Family: Gershon, Anna, Jack, Sam, Mrs Caplan, Carl, Louis and Etty.

Glossary of Yiddish words, phrases and expressions

The reader should know that most Jewish children of my generation knew, and understand fully, the meaning of such words. These are not in alphabetical order but are simply the most common words used in terms of recurrence and popularity:

Mazeltov (as *Mazel*)	Good luck, congratulations.
Meshugé	Mad.
Meshugener	Mad person.
Shmo (or *Shmuck*)	Fool, idiot, simple. Also *Shmock* (obscene) penis.
Shul	Synagogue.
Gelt	Money.
Ganef	Thief.
Goy	Gentile.
Shikse	Gentile girl.
Shalom	Peace, hullo, goodbye.
Tim-Tam	Very naive. (To my knowledge, only used by Scottish Jews.)
Baitz (pron. 'bites')	Hooligan.
Baitzké	Hooligan (female).
Shabbas	Sabbath.
Oy! or *Oy-Oy!*	Woe (an expression of pain, surprise, fear).
Oy gevalt!	As above, but stronger emotionally.
Landsman	Someone from the same town or area in E. Europe.

Mitzva	A good turn, a favour, a virtuous deed.
Minyan	A quorum (requiring 10 male Jews for a religious service).
Mench	A decent person. One who can be trusted.
L'chayim	A toast – 'To life' or 'To your health'.
Cheder	A room or school wherein Hebrew is taught.
Choleria	This word is related to 'cholera'. A curse! The word is seldom used alone; usually it is phrased thus: 'May you contract cholera'. In Yiddish – *'Zol zu chappen a cholera!'*
Kosher	Having many meanings nowadays. Originally, it referred to food only, i.e. food having passed the very strict dietary Boards. In modern usage: anything legal, above board, clean, untainted, trustworthy.
Naches	Pride, pleasure, joy.
Ich lieb dere	I love you.
Barmitzva	Coming of age. At 13 a Jewish boy enters manhood.
Zai gezunt	Keep well, may you remain in good health.
Emmess	Truth.
Tzorriss	Trouble, despair, anguish.

A useful hint to those who may wish to remember some of the above words: in Yiddish the *ch* sounds harsh – as in the Scottish word 'loch'.

Jews from eastern Europe are of the group called *Ashkenazim*. Jews from Babylon, the Greek islands, Africa, Portugal, Spain, southern France and the Orient are *Sephardim*.